MW00878683

THE MONTESSORI PARENT

126 ACTIVITIES THAT FOSTER TODDLER
INDEPENDENCE—A GUIDE TO PROVIDE A
CHILDHOOD OF LOVE, JOY, AND CONFIDENCE
THROUGH THE MONTESSORI PHILOSOPHY

AMY LEE TERRES

© Copyright 2023 - All rights reserved.

The content contained within this book may not be reproduced, duplicated or transmitted without direct written permission from the author or the publisher.

Under no circumstances will any blame or legal responsibility be held against the publisher, or author, for any damages, reparation, or monetary loss due to the information contained within this book, either directly or indirectly.

Legal Notice:

This book is copyright protected. It is only for personal use. You cannot amend, distribute, sell, use, quote or paraphrase any part, or the content within this book, without the consent of the author or publisher.

Disclaimer Notice:

Please note the information contained within this document is for educational and entertainment purposes only. All effort has been executed to present accurate, up to date, reliable, complete information. No warranties of any kind are declared or implied. Readers acknowledge that the author is not engaged in the rendering of legal, financial, medical or professional advice. The content within this book has been derived from various sources. Please consult a licensed professional before attempting any techniques outlined in this book.

By reading this document, the reader agrees that under no circumstances is the author responsible for any losses, direct or indirect, that are incurred as a result of the use of the information contained within this document, including, but not limited to, errors, omissions, or inaccuracies.

CONTENTS

PART FOUR
NURTURE

INTRODUCTION

Whether you are new to the Montessori world or have considered yourself a Montessori parent for some time now, welcome. The aim here is to provide a reference guide that you can turn to for a variety of topics, as well as over 100 Montessori activities that you can do with your toddler. No matter where you are on your journey, I think it's important that you know without a shadow of a doubt how capable you are as a parent and how lucky your child is to have you. The setup of this book follows the acronym ICAN:

- **I**ntroduction: Introduction to Montessori
- **C**reation: Creating a Prepared Environment
- **A**pplication: Application of the Method
- **N**urture: Nurturing a Love of Learning

You may be here because you are at your wits end with your toddler and desperate to try something—anything that might make a positive change—or you may be a first-time parent with a baby on the way and are exploring options for once you reach the toddler years. Either way, I'm glad you're here, and I know that you can do this! The Montessori method can be adopted by anyone; it is inclusive, not exclusive. You can be a Montessori parent and have your children in a traditional school setting. In fact, sending our children to traditional schools is the only option that a majority of families have, and that is okay. The Montessori philosophy works wherever it is used. There are benefits whether your child is in a Montessori school with a Montessori environment at home or in a traditional school with a Montessori environment when they come home. The "level" at which you are able to incorporate these activities into your child's life does not correlate with the amount of love you have for your child. I will be advocating for the Montessori philosophy, yes, but first and foremost, I am advocating for you as a parent and all the ways that you are enough.

Even just having this book, or any book, to help you on your parenting journey and spending some of your valuable and precious time to read or look through it tells me more than I need to know about your unconditional love for your child or children. If you have your child in a traditional school setting or know that that is the plan for them once they start going to school, I do not want you to feel like you are doing something wrong as a parent or that your child will not be successful. This is far from true! Some parents turn to Montessori philosophy for their child because it is the only thing that seems to work for them; others may use these tools at home more sparingly in order to target a certain behavior issue. Wherever you fall on the spectrum, my hope is that you gain even just one tool to add to your "parenting toolbox." With that said, there are no parenting techniques that are foolproof, or that can guarantee that your child will never again have a meltdown; there are simply too many scenarios and factors that weigh into each moment with your child to be able to accomplish such a feat. But the Montessori Philosophy does stand on solid ground and has thousands of testimonials to its name in regards to significant improvements in child behavior and temperament. Along with success stories of children excelling intellectually beyond their years. The philosophy targets your toddler's natural tendencies and works with their strengths to satisfy their need for autonomy as a human. There are several names you may be familiar with of prominent figures who had Montessori education in some capacity in their school years. Entrepreneurs such as Thomas Edison, Jimmy Wales, Sergey Brin, Larry Page, Will Wright, and Jeff Bezos. Artists such as Taylor Swift, Dakota Fanning, David Blaine, Beyonce Knowles, Sean Combs, Gabriel Marquez, and Yo Yo Ma (Anthony, 2017).

Parents of toddlers and elementary-aged kids have praised Montessori education for helping their children excel academically while also being able to interact with their peers and authority figures with respect. The toddler years can pose a lot of challenges to parents, as they seem to clash with their toddler on a regular basis, even when doing their best to maintain peace throughout the day. Montessori methods for toddlers are able to speak to the child's inner longings that they cannot express for themselves through words. Montessori is not random in its approach to each child but rather based on years of scientific observation of children and what is happening in these early years of life. A Montessori environment for very young children gives your infant or toddler the freedom to safely explore and learn through discovery. Montessori:

- Speaks to individual strengths and personality types
- Nurtures order, concentration, and independence
- Gives freedom within safe limits
- Promotes self-correction and self-regulation
- Helps with social-emotional learning
- Encourages active, life-based learning

As a co-owner of a Montessori school, I have fallen in love with Montessori methods over and over again through the years. Parents and their children come into our facility from a variety of backgrounds and with many different reasons for being there, and it is a tremendous joy to receive consistent feedback from them that they feel plugged into a family unit only after a short time with us. Their children have noticeable changes in behavior as their independence is fostered, and the parents feel more equipped to handle their toddler in ways that don't unintentionally stifle them, which leads to bouts of frustration or even meltdowns. The goal of this book is to equip, which is also one of our daily goals at our Montessori center. As much as we want the children in our facility to be there, we also long for their parents or guardians to be as involved as they can be and to take an active role in their child's education. Any way that they can bring Montessori into their home is highly encouraged.

Sometimes our parents have a hard time knowing where to start or what would be most helpful if they aren't able to incorporate every idea that is out there. That's where the content of this book is meant to help. The activities listed are not meant to make you and your toddler busy or to be burdensome to your schedule but rather to bring about a chance to connect in meaningful, fun, and educational ways that will hopefully produce special memories during their precious toddlerhood. There are gems of information in every chapter that will help guide you in understanding more about your toddler and how they can feel supported by you and thrive as a toddler who is content and respectful instead of marked by tantrums or defiant behavior that they simply must "outgrow." We long for families to look back on the toddler years with fondness and to live in the toddler years with joy instead of an earnestness to see it pass.

PART ONE
INFORMATION

CHAPTER 1

UNDERSTANDING MONTESSORI THEORY

> *Clearly, we have a social duty towards this future man, this man who exists as a silhouette around the child, a duty towards this man of tomorrow. Perhaps a great future leader or a great genius is with us and his power will come from the power of the child he is today. This is the vision which we must have.*

> MARIA MONTESSORI

We are indebted in many ways to those who have gone before us and dedicated much or part of their lives to discoveries that are now common-place, such as the lightbulb, toothpaste, and that putting a piece of bread with your cookies will keep them soft. Maria Montessori dedicated an abundance of time and energy to studying the behaviors and tendencies of children so that she could better understand how they are naturally wired to learn. Thank goodness she didn't keep her discoveries to herself but shared her observations so that (initially) her community could benefit, and now much of the world can benefit. Maria Montessori was born and raised in Italy and was one of the first women to become a physician in the 1890's timeframe. She used her schooling and passion as an educator to become an advocate for children's education based on their needs and natural tendencies and not the one-size-fits-all approach that most school systems still use today. She sought to hone in on what each individual child was doing and scientifically analyze their progress with a variety of stimuli and differing levels of adult intervention. Over time, the disorderly children in the pilot program (the first Casa Dei Bambini) began to have more self-control and to show interest in the activities that Montessori had created on their own accord. She described it as them absorbing their environment.

THE 12 MONTESSORI PRINCIPLES

There are 12 key principles for the Montessori Philosophy; they are listed here for your reference as you incorporate this lifestyle into your home and attempt to align with the vision and education goals—should you deem this to be what is best for your child (*12 Select Principles of Montessori Education - GMN*, n.d.).

- Respect for the Child
- Absorbent Mind
- Sensitive Periods
- Educating the Whole Child
- Focus on Individualized Learning

- Freedom of Movement and Choice
- Prepared Environment
- Promotes Intrinsic Motivation
- Child Independence
- Auto-Education
- Work Periods
- Role of Montessori Guides

What do these principles mean? Here is a summary of the flow of these principles: Respect for the individuality of your child is crucial to the Montessori environment, which is why this approach (or any approach) is your choice as a parent since you can best determine the needs of your child. All children have an absorbent mind, but not all children absorb what's around them in the same way or at the same pace. The third principle, the sensitive period, refers to your child's motivation for learning being at a peak, which can sometimes be noted through a high level of concentration. There is also research showing specific periods for certain developmental stages broken down by age (see more in Chapter 2). Educating your whole child means considering all of their senses as well as their social, emotional, spiritual, and intellectual needs. Children are remarkably capable; focusing on individualized learning allows your child to tap into their innate capabilities and have an active role in their learning. This feeds directly into giving them freedom of movement and choice in a prepared environment so they can explore and learn at their own pace. This then promotes intrinsic motivation, as the child chooses what they will put their time and energy into and is proud of the tasks that they complete. This builds their confidence, independence, and ability to auto-educate themselves. Children are allowed work periods that vary in length depending on the task they are working on and how long they choose to focus on it. Montessori guides or Montessori parents observe the child and encourage them as they navigate the classroom or the world around them, paying close attention to the child's achievements so that they can be presented with more advanced tasks at their appropriate pace.

As a parent, you are an invaluable guide on your child's learning journey. You can facilitate and prepare opportunities for your child to take an active role in their education. This is exciting for both you and your child! Your child has been watching you since they were born; you are their biggest role model and cheerleader. Taking an active role in their education can make a tremendous difference in their outlook on learning. If you were to enroll your child in a Montessori school program, being on the same wavelength as your child's Montessori guide will enhance your child's sense of security and allow them to feel at ease at home and school. That is also valuable for your child in any school with any teacher.

COMMON TERMINOLOGY

Control of Error: As your child endeavors to take on an activity and see it to completion, we want there to be a way for the child to know that they have completed the task successfully or if they need to keep working at it without having to be told by someone else. The task in and of itself will consist of elements to guide the child to a place of sure completion. This means the child will be able to successfully complete an activity and have immediate feedback that fuels their self-esteem.

Indirect Presentation: A child is always learning and taking in information, even in settings that are not specifically aiming to influence the child. That is why, as parents, we must take care to watch what we say and do when our child is around, as they may absorb the information and learn to do it themselves, even if that was not our intent. The content is indirect, but the attention of the child's mind locks in regardless.

Three-Hour Work Cycle: This cycle was observed and charted in regards to how children operated when left uninterrupted and showed extreme predictability in the three-hour time-frame, with children having two peaks and one valley, and then the cycle repeats. Watch for indications of this workflow in your child, even at home.

Work: When a child is concentrated or engrossed in an activity, it mirrors much more closely the behavior of an adult who is working and not what we would think of as playing. The work is extremely fulfilling to the child, and therefore, sets up a natural segue for the child to be satisfied later in life and function in society with contentment and excitement. This term is used more often than "play," but that does not diminish the joy that is experienced in either one.

Learning Explosions: Children are absorbing the environment around them nonstop, and over time, it has been observed that a new skill seems to "explode" out of the child seemingly overnight. It is the expression of a skill that had been internally cultivated until the child was ready to act. Skills such as rolling, crawling, pincer grasping, walking, talking, etc.

Socialization: As noted previously, Montessori classrooms have the children in groups of ages that cover a three-year span, as this has proven to enhance healthy interactions among the children. It creates natural leadership roles where the older ones can help the younger ones, which simultaneously gives the older child a sense of accomplishment while reinforcing previously mastered tasks.

For a more extensive list of Montessori terminology, a website is listed at the end of Chapter 8.

MONTESSORI EDUCATION VS TRADITIONAL EDUCATION

As mentioned in the introduction, there are a variety of reasons why you may not be able to have your child in a Montessori school setting, and that is okay. The differences that will be discussed here between Montessori and traditional schooling are simply meant to be informative. The Montessori approach to your child's education and growth is a holistic one. It takes into consideration more than just the intellectual development of your child but also their social interactions, emotional stability, communication skills, and physical well-being. It is often not sustainable in the traditional classroom setting for the teacher to be able to pay close attention to all of the aspects just listed for each child in their classroom. This is not meant to say *anything* negative about those teachers; their desire to care for the whole child is certainly not lacking! I know several of them personally and can attest to their genuine love and care for their students. However, the traditional classroom setting also has state mandates and requirements that must be met.

The rigidity that is in place makes the environment less flexible, and the reach of the teachers is often limited. Many children are still able to thrive in a traditional classroom setting, but many are not. There is also the question of whether the children who do not seem to present any issues in a traditional setting are truly living up to their full potential; would they be presented with a learning environment that suited their needs differently and have them excel even further? Remember the quote at the opening of this chapter? Maria Montessori argues that we have a social *duty* towards these young minds. Let this not ignite a fear of failure as a parent but rather spur us on to discover all the ways we are equipped to love our children even further. Putting in the effort alone is a "success" in the eyes of your child; you need only be present for their affection to be stirred. You've already won when it comes to them, so be gentle with yourself and know that failure is eons away from being possible.

The Montessori approach aims to be more active than passive when teaching. Beyond providing information and expecting the child to listen, digest, and recall it from memory, there would instead be a way for the child to use their hands and connect their senses to the information so they can absorb it in a way that their mind chooses to. The child would also be allotted the time they need to complete the task and not be moved on to another subject in the name of staying in tune with the school's schedule. The traditional setting relies heavily on the teacher as the agent, whereas Montessori relies on the cues of the student. Another major difference between traditional schools and Montessori schools is how the children are grouped together; in the traditional setting, students will be with other children who are less than a year older or younger in age, while in Montessori, there is a wider gap. Classrooms will span over a three-year period, such as 0–3, 3–6, 6–9, 9–12, 12–15, and 15–18. The curriculum is adaptable to the student in Montessori, whereas the student must adapt to the curriculum and pace in a traditional school setting. The five areas of learning are: sensorial, practical life, math, culture, and language.

Take a moment to reflect on your parenting approach using the table below, remembering that one side or the other is not a reflection of "wrong" or "right" but simply different options and approaches towards your child. You know your child best, and there may be scenarios where a typical Montessori parent does something more reflective of traditional education and vice versa. This exercise may help show the applicability of the Montessori approach if you are new to the philosophy and looking to incorporate it into your home.

Traditional	Montessori
• Step in to help when my child takes a while to complete a task	• Give my child ample time to complete a task without aid
• Explain or show a task one way	• Explain or show a task in multiple ways or orders
• Mostly keep my child with other children close in age	• Allow my child access to older and younger children regularly
• Offer external rewards for completed tasks	• Allow the completed task to be my child's reward
• Advocate for my child to learn things that are "typical" for his age	• Give my child a chance to set her pace and discover interests
Notes	

With all the benefits that have been shown through the Montessori method, there is no harm that could be done by simply giving it a try if you are on the fence about whether it would be helpful in your home. Some may be prepared and convinced enough to begin a full remodel of their home, while others may want to incorporate a thing or two to test the waters first. Both approaches are loving and mindful of their children. If your child is toddler age or soon to be toddler age, the next chapter takes a dive into what makes many parents describe this timeframe as difficult. The toddler stage is when your child is learning to self-regulate; this is matched with communication abilities that are still maturing and a longing for independence that, in some ways, cannot be obtained due to their sheer size and/or lack of knowledge about the world around them. Understanding the Montessori philosophy gives us a launching pad for fostering your toddlers' growing inde-pendence.

CHAPTER 2
FOSTERING INDEPENDENCE AND SELF-DIRECTED LEARNING

> *The children of today will make all the discoveries of tomorrow. All the discoveries of mankind will be known to them and they will improve what has been done and make fresh discoveries. They must make all the improvements in houses, cities, communication, methods of production, etc. that are to be made. The future generation must not only know how to do what we can teach them, they must be able to go a step further.*
>
> MARIA MONTESSORI

Your toddler needs practical life skills. At this tender age, activities such as dressing and caring for oneself may take longer and may not be done perfectly when conducted without parental assistance, but your child's craving for this kind of independence is a beautiful part of their development. What is so wrong with wearing a shirt backwards anyways? Toddlers are still limited in their abilities to verbally communicate with precision, which can present a challenge in understanding exactly what they desire. This can lead to frustration not just for the puzzled adult but for the child as well, and since the child is also still developing emotional stability, the frustration they feel can lead to a meltdown or tantrum. Or, the parent may know precisely what their toddler wants but not allow them to have it or do it because of safety reasons, the timing not being appropriate, or a myriad of other reasons that the toddler cannot comprehend. Let me share two stories: the first is one of my parental fails, and the second is one of my friend's parental wins.

When my son was just over two years old, there was an afternoon when he was standing on a stool at the kitchen sink, filling his cup with water. He began to lean to turn the water off once it was full, and I peeked over my shoulder and noticed that the grip on his cup was insufficient and that the amount he needed to lean to reach the faucet would cause him to drop it. I attempted to swoop in and give the bottom of his cup a small amount of support, but I was coming from a strange angle, reaching mostly backwards, and began to lose my balance. In order to stabilize myself, my hand had to go past my son's chest to the other side of the sink, and my finger barely nipped the handle of a pot in the drying rack, but it caused several drying dishes to loudly tumble down onto the counter and one aluminum coffee mug to hit the ground with a sizzling smack.

This unexpected commotion frightened my son, and his arms jerked upwards, throwing his water-filled cup into the nearby wall! Had I not interfered, the worst that would have happened was my son's plastic cup falling a couple of inches into the sink and needing to be refilled. Instead, I scared my son, nearly knocked him off the stool, created a mess, and unintentionally stifled him in a moment where he would have been able to learn on his own that he needed a stronger grip on his cup. My actions did not foster independence or self-directed learning whatsoever.

Now for a win. I recall observing my friend, a mother of her 20-month-old daughter at the time, find a rock in the front yard that was covered in dirt. They made their way to the water hose, turned it on, and rinsed the rock off. All was well in the world until the mother twisted the knob to stop the flow of water, and her toddler indicated respectfully that she wished to continue rinsing the rock, so the mother obliged, thinking she would likely be content with another minute. A minute passed... Three minutes passed... And her daughter stood holding her rock under the flow of water, simply mesmerized by the experience. Meanwhile, a sizable puddle was being created in the grass, and the mother knew this wasn't conducive to conserving water during the peak of summer, and that water was not free, but she also knew that her daughter was displaying concentration that she didn't want to have to bring to an end, which would also likely result in a meltdown. So mom quickly put her knowledge of Montessori activities into action to save the day. She gently pulled her toddler's attention off the rock and water to tell her she could go find more dirty rocks to be washed. She used that buffer to find and fill a medium-sized bin halfway with water and place a cup inside. Her daughter returned, and we were able to observe as she engaged in not just happily cleaning rocks but refining her fine motor skills by using the cup in one hand to accurately pour the water over the rock in her other hand. This fostered independence and self-directed learning.

WHAT IS A TODDLER?

There are discrepancies between scholars in defining the age of a "toddler," but the most common range agreed upon is from ages 1–3. On average, this is what a toddler is capable of:

- **Emotionally**: Toddlers are able to experience a wide range of emotions, from sadness, fear, and disgust to joy, pride, and excitement. They begin to express themselves through assertiveness or even demands (verbally or physically) when they are experiencing negative emotions and express themselves through laughter, affection, or not being able to stay still when they are on the positive side. They are also able to start picking up on the emotions of those around them through the use of tone, which they will also be able to start using more effectively around age two.

- **Socially**: Before age one, babies are able to tell the difference between a stranger and someone familiar to them and may start to show a preference for those they know, especially once they reach a year. They may become more closed off socially and show a strong preference for family members over strangers (many label this as separation anxiety), or they may take well to anyone who is in the room and not have a strong reaction to their caregivers being far from them for short periods of time. Toddlers will often use their skill of pointing at things to interact with others and express themselves. A predominant interaction with other children at this age may consist of a lot of protectiveness of their toys, laughing at each other's laughter, and reaching out to touch each other or eventually to give hugs.

- **Mentally**: The brain of a three-year-old is 80% developed and houses a large amount of data for language, reasoning, and memory. In this 1–3-year time span, they will go from saying singular words to stringing together short, simple sentences and from shaking rattles to stacking towers and completing puzzles.
- **Physically**: Toddlers can walk, climb, jump, run, dance, stretch, kick, hit, talk, color, eat with a spoon, and more.

The attention span of toddlers is typically 2–8 minutes, but Montessori-inspired activities have yielded exciting results in this regard when children get locked in on an activity and are determined to see it through to completion. Montessori guides try not to interrupt a child who is clearly engrossed in what they are doing. This allows the child to maintain focus for as long as necessary and increases their attention span. This toddler timeframe of seeking independence is wired into them; they cannot help but have the drive to learn to do things for themselves. Letting them do the things they are trying to do to help themselves or to help others is growing them in many positive ways, including their self-esteem, awareness, cognitive function, sense of belonging, and overall well-being. As Maria

Montessori put it, "Never do for the child what he/she can do for himself/herself." A great place to start is to consider your child's senses and utilize activities that expound upon their taste, touch, sight, hearing, and smell. This is called "sensory play," and it is important and acceptable to introduce it to your child, even as a newborn. Sensory play has benefits for growing your toddler's fine motor skills, supporting their memory, problem-solving, general understanding of the world around them, and encouraging creativity (Action for Children, 2022). The term "Sensitive Periods" is something you hear about on a regular basis in the Montessori world. It refers primarily to ages 0–3, but all the way up to 0–6, where our children have been observed to experience "transient periods of sensibility, and are intrinsically motivated or urged to activity by specific sensitivities. A child in a sensitive period is believed to exhibit spontaneous concentration when engaged in an activity that matches their particular sensitivity. For example, children in a sensitive period for order will be drawn to activities that involve ordering. They will be observed choosing such activities and becoming deeply concentrated, sometimes repeating the activity over and over without external reward or encouragement. Young children are naturally drawn towards those specific aspects of the environment that meet their developmental needs" Association Montessori Internationale (n.d.).

The six sensitive periods observed and capitalized on through the Montessori Philosophy are:

1. Movement: Birth to four years old
2. Language: Birth to six years old

3. Sensorial Exploration: Birth to six years old
4. Small Objects: Three months to four years old
5. Order: Six months to three years old
6. Social Interaction: About two to six years old and up

Your toddler wants to move, talk, explore with all their senses, handle small objects with ease, and feel secure in a routine and a community. Beyond that, they need to accomplish and discover these periods for themselves. The guardians around a toddler cannot be the ones to determine when they have satisfied their needs in each category; only the child can determine that. This doesn't mean you don't play a role as a parent; you most certainly do! You can provide an ample amount of external stimuli and opportunities for your child to flourish in all of these areas and keep a close eye on their accomplishments to better aid their progression. Especially with the Order stage and Social Interaction stage, you play a key role in making sure your child has a predictable schedule and flow to their day when they are home, just like they do on the days that they are at school. You can also set up playdates with other children and schedule visits with family members near and far to help them establish their sense of community and that they belong and are loved wherever they are in this big world. Case studies have begun to show that children involved in Montessori schooling in their childhood, even if just for two years, have a higher level of well-being as adults (Lillard, 2021). Recent studies of the brain have shown that they align with the beliefs of Maria Montessori and the theories she used as the basis for her schooling methods with children. Especially as it pertains to external rewards for toddlers accomplishing tasks that otherwise could feel rewarded through the pride of completing the task and not for the tangible reward provided by the parents or teacher. The Montessori method facilitates a chance for the child to build confidence in themselves, and other forms using external rewards teach the child to look outward instead of inward for approval. External rewards have their place and can be used wisely and properly to avoid detrimental effects on the psychology of our young children, but unfortunately, it is commonplace to use external rewards today instead of being more scarce.

LANGUAGE ACQUISITION + ACTIVITIES

It is quite magical to watch a child go from an infant babble to a toddler forming sentences. It can also be humorous as they learn to pronounce words accurately, as well as frustrating when no one can seem to understand what this little person is trying so desperately to say. At this age, toddlers learn to speak by listening to the adults and older children around them and observing the shape and movements of their mouths. Much of language acquisition is indirect since the adult cannot force the child to move their mouth or tongue in the proper way or assist them in vibrating their vocal cords. However, there are still plenty of ways you can take on an active role as your toddler learns to speak and grows their vocabulary. This can be done through storytelling, reading, or intentional conversation. It is important to remember that even between adults, a large majority of communication is nonverbal and expressed through tone, facial expressions, and body language. Your child will be picking up on all of these nonverbal cues as well and be able to communicate in ways that are beyond the use of words, such as hugs and kisses or crossed arms and a furrowed brow. Helping your toddler name the emotions they are feeling is one of the first steps to guiding them down a path of healthy conflict resolution. There is a large amount of research and tools for conflict resolution that are relatively new. Because of this, there are many adults who are not equipped with these skills or who did not grow up learning them. If you fall into this category, I highly recommend digesting some of the research for yourself and applying it to your interactions with your significant other, kids, friends, and other family members. Our children are much more inclined to do what they see us doing than just being told "this is the way" without seeing it displayed for them. Help your child label their emotions; teach them that emotions are not bad and that we can talk about what we feel with other people so that they can help us if we are struggling with sadness, fear, or anger. Teach them that pausing what they are doing to talk about their feelings should come first so that behavior like hitting or screaming at their friend (or at you) can be avoided (Engler, 2021).

Effective communication must also include listening—just as your toddler is learning to talk by observing you; they are also learning to be a good listener by observing you. All of the same active listening skills you know as an adult are applicable to your interactions with your toddler, namely, eye contact, affirmation sounds or words, nodding, repeating back what you think you heard, and not being distracted. When we practice active listening, we are able to key in on more than just the words our toddler is trying to say, but also on ways that they are calling out to us that they are striving for independence, which gives us clues to how we can optimize the moment to help them down that path. Some of the differences between communicating with fellow adults or older children and your toddler are over-inflecting and talking about *every*thing. It would be a little odd to declare to another adult, "You are filling your cup with water. Do you know what color your cup is? That's right, it's yellow. Yeh-yeh-yellow." Although this type of interaction is incredibly beneficial for your toddler. Overemphasizing, over-inflecting, over-pronouncing, and repeating your words helps toddlers mimic the sounds and attempt to form their lips and tongue in proper ways. Taking opportunities to talk through all the things your little one is doing or the things that are happening around them exposes them to more sounds, more vocabulary, and more opportunities to practice. Making sounds in general, not necessarily words, is also a crucial part of your child's language development as it exercises and stretches their vocal cords. This can be done by mimicking the sounds that animals or motor vehicles make. There are many activities you can utilize to engage with your toddler as they acquire more language but remember that it can also be as simple as being present with your child and letting them hear your voice.

#1 **Activity**: Name Everything

Age Group: 1+

Materials Needed: None

What To Do: Point to objects around the house, car, park, doctor's office, or wherever you are and tell your child what it is. See if they can repeat it back to you.

#2 **Activity**: Describe Everything

Age Group: 1+

Materials Needed: None

What To Do: Beyond telling your child what items are called, discuss what color they are, how big or small they are, what they do, and anything about the object that calls to their senses (taste, smell, sound, touch, and sight).

#3 **Activity**: Sing Together

Age Group: 0+

Materials Needed: None

What To Do: Sing! Sing songs you know, or make up songs about what you are currently doing with your child.

#4 **Activity**: Rhyming

Age Group: 2.5+

Materials Needed: None

What To Do: Provide your child with a word and see how many rhymes they can make with it, i.e., look: book, took, shook, hook, crook, cook, etc. This can lead to them learning the meaning of unfamiliar words. *Note:* Be careful with the words you choose if your child starts trying random letters and ends up with a curse word, i.e., luck or hit.

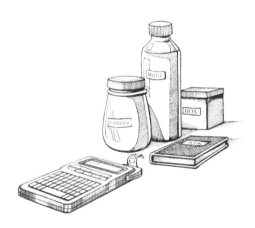

#5 **Activity**: Label Everything

Age Group: 2.5+

Materials Needed: A label maker if you have one and prefer to use it, or paper, markers, and tape to create your own.

What to Do: Okay, maybe not *every*thing, but you get the idea. This activity is great to start once your toddler shows more interest in reading and identifying letters.

#6 **Activity**: Read Together

Age Group: 6 months+

Materials Needed: Children's books

What to Do: Hold your child or sit down close to them and read a book. Let them look at the pictures and touch the pages if appropriate. With children over age one, remember to watch their cues for concentration and let them linger on a page if they so desire. Talk about the pictures in the book beyond just reading the words from the pages; ask open-ended questions to ensure they are following the story.

#7 **Activity**: Storytelling

Age Group: 1+

Materials Needed: None

What to Do: Similar to reading together, except you are just talking to your child and either making up a story or telling them a true story about something that has happened (family history, something funny while you were at work that day, etc.). Encourage your child to make up their own story, make a combined story together, or tell you about the things they did that day.

#8 **Activity**: Tracing Letters

Age Group: 4+

Materials Needed: Writing utensils, paper

What to Do: Write out the alphabet in uppercase and lowercase letters with plenty of space between each letter. Your child will come behind you and trace over the letters with their own writing utensil. There are also several great options out there for writing practice that you can look into, such as workbooks that have grooves in the paper where the letters are to help keep your child steady and on track.

#9 **Activity**: Exposure to Other Languages

Age Group: 0+

Materials Needed: None

What to Do: If there is any possibility of your child being exposed to a second language on a regular basis, do it. Babies speak all languages! If there is a family member or the possibility of a nanny that can be present to speak a second language and ensure comprehension and proper pronunciation in those first few years of life, it is extremely valuable to the child. Learning a new language to the point of proficiency only increases in difficulty the older a person gets, yet for a baby, it is effortless. If you yourself speak more than one language, do all you can to bless your child with that as well. Yes, it will require effort and consistency for a number of years, but your child will reap the benefits for the rest of their life.

SELF-CARE SKILLS + ACTIVITIES

Planning ahead is helpful. Letting your child do things for themselves *will* take longer than if you did them for them. Account for this fact in your day-to-day life so that you can be up with your child with enough time to let them attempt to do things on their own before it's imperative to be out the door. You can also set boundaries, such as telling your toddler that they have X amount of minutes to work on putting on their shoes, and then mommy will help them if still needed. This also allows them to self-motivate and work on concentration. If you aren't going to be leaving the house but don't want your child to spend an endless amount of time getting dressed, then rely on the structure you have in place for the flow of days that are spent at home. This could look like your child knowing the routine is to wake up, go potty, get dressed, and brush their hair before being able to come to eat breakfast.

Children thrive on structure and routine. Having a flow to the day minimizes the chance of the child feeling insecure or confused about what is expected of them. Along with planning ahead and setting boundaries for your child to try these skills on their own, it can also be helpful to limit their options of what they can choose to put on or make it a part of their bedtime routine to pick out their clothes for the next day. Talk about the tags, pockets, and other identifiers they can look for on their clothing to know if it is the front or back.

When it comes to eating, allow your child to practice picking up food from their tray and bringing it to their mouth starting at a very young age, about six or seven months. Expose them to as many veggies and fruits as you can; try to expand their palate as much as possible before they turn one. Undressing them down to their diaper will help keep clothes cleaner, but be okay with the fact that the high chair, floor, and your child will get messy and need cleaning up. Be present with the baby spoon to ensure some of it does make it into their system, but know that a good amount might be in many places besides their mouth, and that is great! They are learning so much even if all the food isn't being consumed.

Homes do not typically have kid-friendly counter heights, so investing in a stool or two for your little ones will be money well spent. This way, they can reach the sink faucets and be able to practice washing their hands, brushing their teeth, looking into the mirror to brush their hair, and other bathroom activities. While bathing, your toddler will need to learn to scrub the shampoo into their scalp, rinse their hair, and ensure that all their nooks and crannies are cleaned with soap. For their safety, you will need to be present during bathtime for quite some time, but they can still practice these skills on their own and use objects like a cup to pour water over their head or a washcloth to clean their ears and in between their toes. Around age one, when your child coughs or sneezes, you can begin manually moving their arm to bring their inner elbow over their mouth and say, "Cover your mouth." This will be repeated for many days, but your toddler will begin to do it on their own as well as remember to say, "Excuse me," for burps and gas.

Toddlers learning to dress and care for themselves with personal hygiene, and feed themselves are all activities that require fine motor skills and promote cognitive function, so we want them to practice and master these daily activities. Be proud of the progress they make and encourage them as they move in the right direction with each skill. Children do not meet all milestones at the exact same time, especially in the first 12 months of life; therefore, refrain from comparing your little ones to others or blaming yourself for them not hitting milestones precisely when the internet says so. Some children will hold out in the mental preparation stage for certain skills longer than others; this is not something you can force the child to do more quickly; they will reach a place of readiness when it is right in their amazing and unique brain.

The term *Exercises of Practical Life* is explained in this way: "One of the four areas of activities of the Montessori-prepared environment. The exercises of Practical Life resemble the simple work of life in the home: sweeping, dusting, washing dishes, etc. These purposeful activities help the child adapt to his new community, learn self-control, and begin to see himself as a contributing member of the social unit. His intellect grows as he works with his hands; his personality becomes integrated as body and mind function as a unit" (Association Montessori Internationale, n.d.).

#10 **Activity**: Create a Routine and Checklist

Age Group: 2+

Materials Needed: Construction paper, markers, a ruler, and about 10–20 small magnets. *Alternatives:* Use a small whiteboard and expo markers; create an Excel spreadsheet and print it out.

What to Do: This can be as simple or elaborate as you desire. Use the materials to write out what a typical day at home will look like, broken down by the hour. Your child should be able to understand what activities follow others, i.e., wake up and prepare for the day, followed by breakfast, then playtime, clean up, lunch, nap, playtime, clean up, dinner, prepare for bed, storytime, bedtime. You can make a more general chart of the routine that is then broken down into more specifics, such as a checklist of what your child is to complete or accomplish during "Wake up and prepare for the day." Create two columns, one that says "incomplete" and one that says "complete," with a list such as go potty, brush hair, brush teeth, put on clothes, put pajamas away, and make bed. If you keep your chart on the fridge or another place that is magnet-friendly, your child can move the magnet from "incomplete" to "complete."

#11 **Activity**: Button, Zip, and Tie

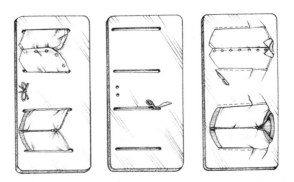

Age Group: 2+

Materials Needed: A medium to large piece of cardboard or a smooth, thin wooden board; a knife, scissors, or potentially a hand or table saw if you are using more sturdy wood; a pencil or pen; a zip-up jacket of any size; a button-up flannel of any size; and shoelaces—these can be old items from your house that never get used, or you can purchase cheap ones from a thrift store.

What to Do: Lay your chosen board material flat on the floor and lay the zipped-up jacket and buttoned-up flannel down next to each other on the board. Mark the board along the left and right sides of each piece of clothing, from the armpit down to the hem. Remove the clothing and use a proper tool to cut a thin opening along the line you made. Ensure that the opening is just wide enough to be able to pull the fabric of the jacket and flannel through. Place the board facing down on the ground and work the jacket and flannel through their respective openings. Turn the board back over and continue pulling the left and right sides of the clothing through the openings. Your child can now practice zipping up the jacket and buttoning up the flannel as many times as they want. You can also make two holes in any extra space on the board to put a shoelace through (thick string or yarn could be an alternative). Your child can practice tying knots and bows. If you have extra space on your board, you can add other things, such as a strip of Velcro, to have more things for your child to experience.

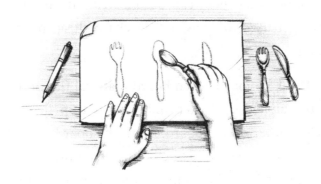

#12 **Activity**: Spoons, Forks, and Knives

Age Group: 1.5+

Materials Needed: Paper, marker or pen, baby spoon, baby fork, baby knife (toy utensils or their real baby utensils are fine)

What to Do: Trace each utensil on the paper and set it in front of your toddler with the utensils for them to match them up correctly. If they bring the utensils to their mouth, that is fine; you can work with them to hold the correct end and practice bringing it to their mouth.

#13 **Activity**: Matching Outfits

Age Group: 2.5+

Materials Needed: Prints of individual and animated pieces of clothing of a variety of colors and styles (shirts, dresses, pants, shorts, shoes, hats, etc.), scissors, a whiteboard, and a pack of peel-and-stick magnets.

What to Do: Cut the printouts into individual squares for each piece of clothing, secure a peel-and-stick magnet to the back of each one, and place them on a whiteboard or other magnet-friendly surface. Your child can mix and match the items to create different outfits. You can talk with your child about what makes their outfit match or not match. You can also do this when picking out their real outfits to wear.

#14 **Activity**: Shoes

Age Group: 2+

Materials Needed: Your child's shoes, stickers, scissors

What to Do: Velcro shoes are simpler when starting off. To help with identifying between the right and the left, you can get stickers that are about the size of a quarter, cut one in half, place the left side on your child's left shoe near the big toe area, and place the right half of the sticker on the right shoe so that when you line the shoes up next to each other, the sticker looks to be complete. You can also look into weaving a bead onto shoelaces that have an "L" and an "R" once they recognize letters and understand the concept of left and right a bit more.

#15 **Activity**: Practice Dressing

Age Group: 2+

Materials Needed: Daily clothes

What to Do: Let your child practice; give them time and space to work without distractions; limit their choices; use clothes that are not extremely fitted so they have space to get their arms and legs through more easily.

#16 **Activity**: Potty Training Tip

Age Group: 1.5+

Materials Needed: None

What to Do: Talk and show! The first step to potty training is bringing your child to a cognitive awareness of their bodily functions. Talk openly: "Mommy needs to go potty now." Let your child see that you are sitting on the toilet. When you are changing diapers, talk about what it is that has occurred inside their diaper; get them interested in this abstract notion of "going potty."

#17 **Activity**: Hair Brushing Practice

Age Group: 2.5+

Materials Needed: Hairbrush and enough hair on someone's head (preferably an adult)

What to Do: If you have hair that comes down at least to your shoulders or so, you can use your head for your child's hair-brushing practice. I highly recommend brushing through your hair *first* to remove all tangles and to avoid pain during this activity. Sit down in front of your child and give them your hairbrush so they can brush your hair. Talk to them about being gentle, and then work with them on holding the brush in the other direction so they can run it through their own hair.

#18 **Activity**: Brushing Teeth

Age Group: 1.5+

Materials Needed: Children's toothbrush, toothpaste, and a two-minute timer

What to Do: You will need to be a part of your child's tooth brushing practice for a while to ensure that they are doing it sufficiently. It will start with holding their hand as they hold their toothbrush, guiding it where it will go, and controlling the pressure. Over time, ease up little by little on how much you are controlling their movements while still monitoring and talking to them about scrubbing the front and back of every tooth and not forgetting their tongue. Use the timer to ensure they are cleaning for long enough. There are toothbrushes that have fun features like sounds and lights to aid in this development as well.

SELF-DIRECTED PLAY

Another important part of fostering your toddler's independence is through self-directed play. Having a safe environment for your toddler to play without any specific activity as their guide helps them build creativity and explore the world on their own. Open play in the Montessori environment is not drastically different from traditional open play. The only factor that typically differs is how Montessori philosophy focuses on real life and not as much on fairy tales and make-believe. Montessori classrooms look a lot like smaller versions of kitchens and offices that adults utilize. Outdoor play is also highly encouraged. This time in a child's day is to be pressure-free and fun, but since children are almost always in a state of learning, they can still be observed exhibiting high levels of concentration during self-directed play, which is a sign of a content child.

PART TWO
CREATION

CHAPTER 3
YOUR MONTESSORI HOME

> *The absorption of the environment is an intellectual activity. It is a psychic necessity that the child explores the environment; it satisfies his spirit. After he has had the satisfaction of observing one thing that interests him, he goes on until he is attracted by something else. In this way, the child can walk for miles.*

MARIA MONTESSORI

The Brugge Family: Dad is a mechanic and often works on vehicles out of their personal garage. There are many different tools necessary in this line of work, and the garage was beginning to turn into a maze. Their two-year-old son loves to "work" with dad, but mom is unable to take her eyes off him as he follows dad around and shows interest in the tools that could be a danger to him. If mom cannot watch him due to needing to prepare dinner or other obligations, then dad isn't able to actually work since their son could get himself into a mess. This couple set up a weekend for their son to spend with the grandparents so they could clean out and organize the garage. They installed shelving and storage high enough for curious fingers not to be able to reach, but in one corner, they installed a gated area with an oversized activity board of tools, tool parts, and miscellaneous equipment that was safe for their son to tinker and "work" with while still having a view of what dad was up to.

The Tucker Family: Mom is an artist in her spare time in the spare bedroom who especially loves to work with paint. As her son has learned to walk and show more control with his hands, he often asks if they can paint. Mom loved the idea of being able to paint together in the same room while still working independently. She ordered a baby gate that had panels that could be rearranged in a number of different ways and set it up as a long rectangle against one of the open walls in her workroom. She covered the wall in long strips of paper in any areas her son could reach, as well as the vinyl flooring in the gated area. She then secured a roll of paper on the wall at one end of the gated area and pulled the paper to the other end. This way, her son could get paint on any area without it being an issue, and they could spend time together chatting while they created masterpieces. This also made for easy cleanup, as she could simply remove the old paper and replace it whenever necessary.

The Steel Family: This family has five kids in the age range of one to nine. They are blessed to have a multi-purpose room in their house that is oversized and versatile. They have utilized baby gates to section the room in a way that creates four spaces. Each space has toys and equipment for a different age group, so all the children can be in one room without trampling over one another or having to be separated in their rooms across the house. They can play together or independently, and the older kids can navigate through the gates to help the younger ones when necessary.

A PREPARED ENVIRONMENT

The Montessori concepts within the home are extremely adaptable, so you can create spaces that work for your family. The ways in which exploration, independence, and a love for learning are promoted will look differently between homes so that they fit the needs and work with what each family has. A prepared environment is the goal. Research has proven that our physical environment has an effect on us mentally and emotionally. Physical chaos and clutter entail mental chaos and clutter, while physical cleanliness and organization yield the same mentally. This is part of taking on Montessori philosophy that takes the most thought and effort on your end; it may also require some money, but much can be accomplished even on the smallest of budgets. Many have heard the saying, "A place for everything and everything in its place." This falls right in line with the goal of a prepared environment. Decluttering is a joyous experience for some (guilty!), but for others, it can be dreadful. If you're currently breaking out in a sweat reading this, take a deep breath, and please keep reading. You *can* do this, and you will reap the benefits just as much as your family! It is worth it to coordinate a weekend… or week… to have someone care for your children so that you and your significant other or any close family or friends can dedicate some time to getting things in order. If you're confident that you can get it done without sending your kids away, that's fine too. Whatever works for your family.

It truly is astonishing how quickly we accumulate things. I've found a common thread among several of the Montessori parents that I know in that we all seem to have a mental inventory of our possessions and have created unspoken routines for removing excess throughout the year. If you ask us, "Do you have any green thread?" We would know immediately yes or no and exactly where it is being stored. Many of my friends can attest that they did not reach this place overnight or easily. It took time and dedication, but once they found their flow, it turned into "routine maintenance" and was a lot easier.

SIMPLICITY, ORDER, AND KID-FRIENDLINESS

Strive for simplicity and order in the layout of your home. Think about what is accessible to your kids and what is not. If you store things out of their reach, let it be done intentionally for the purpose of facilitating their environment by rotating between toys every few weeks and which clothes they are allowed to choose from to wear. If you know anything about minimalism, those concepts all fit very nicely with Montessori philosophy. It has also been noted that Montessori classrooms are filled with quality wood furniture, toys, and materials instead of a lot of bright colors and plastics (Viktoria, 2020). The choice of natural tones over bold colors is to promote an environment where the child is able to concentrate on their activity and is not easily distracted by their surroundings.

Child-sized furniture enables a sense of calm for your child; the furniture is not intimidating or challenging for them to utilize. Miniature kitchens with miniature kitchen materials are a space where a child can explore without difficulty. Open shelving allows the child to see their options and choose something that catches their attention. Any options for incorporating natural materials into your home are encouraged. When it comes to toys, be picky. Strive to incorporate toys that mimic real-life materials or that serve a purpose in supporting your child's development in some form or fashion. The hardest part of this can often be around your child's birthday or gift-giving holidays. Try including a friendly note on invitations that encourages those desiring to bestow a gift on your little one to consider experience-based gifts (a trip to the zoo, going out for ice cream, visiting the local botanical garden) or gift cards in place of toys. Thank them for considering such generosity towards your child. Attempt to have an open dialogue with family members about your goals with the Montessori philosophy so they can be more understanding of how things might change around your house and why. There are many ways for them to give gifts that align with the heart behind Montessori methods.

Create specific learning spaces for your child. A designated area for arts and crafts, reading, a puzzle nook, a free-play zone, a practical life activities space, and so on. Whether you live in an apartment or on several acres of land, know where you can go to let your child safely explore outside. Remember to bring nature into your home as well with potted plants, hanging plants, or low-maintenance plants.

As your child reaches the end of toddlerhood, start involving them in the organization choices in their bedroom and play areas so you can discuss with them the reasoning behind keeping their spaces clutter-free and how it links together with having a clutter-free mind. Talk about how we want our minds to be open and available for all the many things that are out there for us to learn, not hampered by a physical mess around us and unable to soak in information. Allow them to take ownership of simple areas, like a shelf for their stuffed animals or building a rack with dad so they can organize hats or bows.

Choose a few things from this list that you would like to do or incorporate into your home. Don't make it overwhelming; it is okay to start small, and over time, you can add more.

	Declutter		Limit access to clothes		Incorporate natural tones
	Organize toys		Rotate between clothes		Bring some nature inside
	Use open shelving		Have step stools to use		Choose a go-to nature spot
	Use child-sized furniture		Limit screen time		Simplify your spaces
	Use wooden products		Use floor mats		Allow for natural light
	Limit access to toys		Reduce external rewards		Create specific learning areas
	Rotate between toys		Use baby gates		Avoid toys with batteries
	Use baskets and trays		Allow space for movement		Strive for a calm space
	Use a mini kitchen		Have low shelving		Create a book display
	Child-sized cleaning tools		Potty training seat		A place for everything

MATERIALS

Before we dive into activities in the coming chapters, it is good to note that there are certain materials that are used often enough that it is wise to simply keep them on hand. If you've always dreamed of a craft closet or space, now is the time to bring that dream to fruition. The aim of the activities in this book is to be manageable with common household materials so that you can utilize them on the spot without needing to drop a lot of money on supplies ahead of time. There will be a few activities that require more preparation than others. Any of these activities can be improved upon using more sturdy or lasting materials if that is what you so desire. Any chance to reuse or recycle materials is encouraged as well. The goal was to make these activities as accessible as possible so you can bring the essence of Montessori into your home without breaking the bank or draining an excess amount of your treasured time. Any way you can use natural materials and wood is a bonus and appropriate for the Montessori environment, but the ultimate goal here is not to turn your home into a secondary Montessori classroom, because in fact, it already *is* one! The goal is to optimize your home space to include your toddler as much as possible so their growing independence can be fostered and nurtured. Below you will find a list of general materials that tend to be on repeat for a lot of the activities or that can aid in creating your own. DIY is highly encouraged; you'll be amazed at the ideas you can come up with and by the ideas of your child!

Some basics one might find in a Neatly-Organized-Dreamy-Craft-Closet:

- Scissors
- Painters Tape
- Duct Tape
- Regular Tape
- Double Sided Tape
- Liquid Glue
- Glue Sticks
- Hot Glue Gun
- Access to a Printer
- Regular and Colored Printer Paper
- Construction Paper
- Cardstock
- Index Cards
- Markers and Sharpies
- Colored Pencils
- Pencils
- Pens
- Crayons
- Small, Medium, and Large Containers
- Buckets
- Baskets
- Broken Down Cardboard Boxes
- A Collection of Newspaper
- Yarn, String, Ribbon
- Thin Rope
- Shoe Laces
- Empty Toilet Paper and Paper Towel Rolls

- Rolls of Paper
- Paint Brushes
- Paint
- Ruler
- Measuring Tape
- Stamps and Stickers
- Chalk
- Beads
- Label Maker
- Wooden dowel rods
- Wooden Blocks
- Miscellaneous Wooden Materials

CHAPTER 4
NATURAL EXPLORATION

> *It is not enough to see that the child gets good food, good physical care, and enough sleep, because development needs activity too. Experience in the environment is necessary because everyone must be adapted to the environment.*

MARIA MONTESSORI

SENSORIAL EXPLORATION + ACTIVITIES

Sensorial exploration for your child begins on day one and is a crucial part of their development that affects their cognitive function and ability to concentrate. Typically, we think of only our five main senses, but humans are able to experience the world in many more sensorial ways.

Here are ten senses to think about:

1. Visual: Learning to differentiate, draw similarities between, and categorize objects and people
2. Tactical: Sense of touch, especially in the fingertips
3. Baric: Pressure and weight
4. Thermic: Distinguish and develop a sense of temperature
5. Auditory: Differentiating between sounds and noticing variations
6. Olfactory: Exploring one's sense of smell
7. Gustatory: Sense of taste
8. Stereognostic: Sometimes described as muscle memory, it identifies objects without relying on other senses, such as sight
9. Vestibular: Balance and movement
10. Proprioceptive: Positions of body parts, coordination between them, and how much force to use

As your child explores their senses and begins to master tasks, their confidence grows, and they satisfy their appetite for independence bit by bit. Every activity in this book will draw on your child's senses in some way, but there are certain activities you can do to specifically focus on sensorial exploration in order to heighten your child's senses. In the Montessori world, you will likely hear about these most commonly used sensorial activities:

- The Pink Tower: Ten wooden cubes that increase in size by even increments and stack on top of one another to create a tower.
- Brown Stairs: Ten square prisms that increase in size by even increments, when lined up correctly, create a miniature staircase.
- Knobbed Cylinders: Blocks of wood with approximately ten knobbed cylinders each, or varying sizes, must fit into their corresponding hole in the block.
- Geometric Solids: A set of wooden shapes consisting of a cylinder, cube, triangular prism, rectangular prism, sphere, cone, triangular-based pyramid, ellipsoid, ovoid, and square-based pyramid.

Below are a few activities to get you started on your child's sensory explorations; there are many more in Chapters 5 and 6.

#19 **Activity**: Feeling Paint

Age Group: 10 months+

Materials Needed: Snack-sized ziplock bags and various colors of paint

What to Do: Put 3–4 squirts of one color of paint into a ziplock bag and squeeze the air out while closing; repeat for each color of paint. Place the sealed bags in front of your child so they can press on them, and move the paint around inside the bag to explore how it feels and notice the different colors. It is recommended to use washable paint just in case a mess somehow occurs.

#20 **Activity**: Sensory Bin - Pasta

Age Group: 2+

Materials Needed: Large storage container, dry pasta noodles, food coloring, rubbing alcohol, gallon ziplock bags, cookie sheet, and parchment paper

What to Do: Pour a box of pasta into a gallon ziplock bag, mix 10–20 drops of food coloring with one tablespoon of rubbing alcohol or white vinegar, pour into a ziplock bag and seal. Shake the bag and move the pasta around until fully coated. Pour the pasta out onto a parchment-lined baking sheet to dry. Repeat the steps with as many boxes of pasta noodles and colors as desired. Once all of them are dry, pour them into the large storage container. Your child can explore how the pasta feels by moving it around with their hands; they can notice the different shapes of the pasta (if you've used more than one) and the different colors. You can place smaller containers next to the bin for your child to separate the pasta by color or shape.

#21 **Activity**: Sensory Bin - Pasta + Objects

Age Group: 2+

Materials Needed: Large storage container, dry pasta noodles, food coloring, rubbing alcohol, gallon ziplock bags, cookie sheet, parchment paper, and several small to medium-sized toys.

What to Do: Follow the steps in the activity above for dying the pasta. Put the pasta and the toys into the large container so that the toys or objects are hidden. Your child can have a treasure hunt, searching for the toys and pulling them out.

#22 **Activity**: Sensory Bin - Rice

Age Group: 2+

Materials Needed: Medium to large storage containers; smaller containers (quantity to match the amount of colors you use to dye the rice) uncooked rice, food coloring, white vinegar, gallon ziplock bags, a cookie sheet, parchment paper, and a large spoon

What to Do: For every cup of rice, use one teaspoon of white vinegar and 1/8 teaspoon or more of food coloring. Pour the rice with the vinegar and food coloring into a ziplock bag, shake, and move around until fully coated, then pour out onto a parchment-covered baking sheet until dry. Repeat the steps for each color you choose. Keep the colors separated into smaller containers. Supply your child with a large spoon and an empty medium-to-large container. They can use their hands or the spoon to explore the rice and see what happens when they scoop the various colors to be mixed together in the larger container.

#23 **Activity**: Sensory Bin - Rice + Objects

Age Group: 2+

Materials Needed: Large storage container, uncooked rice, food coloring, white vinegar, gallon ziplock bags, a cookie sheet, parchment paper, tongs, and several small toys or objects.

What to Do: Follow the steps in the activity above for dying the rice. Put rice and toys or objects into the large container so that they are hidden. Your child can go on a treasure hunt with their hands, or they can use tongs to retrieve the items from the bin.

FINE MOTOR SKILLS + ACTIVITIES

Fine motor skills not only aid us in many facets of our lives but are also crucial for functioning independently as adults in many ways. In South Korea and other Asian countries, young children are taught to use chopsticks and must practice moving one piece of rice at a time from one plate to another. That is truly honing in on fine motor skills! The sooner your child can control the grasp of their fingers with intentionality and hold onto objects and move them precisely where they desire, the sooner they will be able to achieve all the many feats that they thirst for in regards to being independent. Fine motor skills link directly to cognitive growth as your child begins to understand exactly what all of their fingers, toes, and body parts are capable of doing in order to achieve a desire. For example, if your child wants to eat food and discovers that they can pinch two fingers together on a piece of food and bring it to their mouth, they can hold a spoon or fork and guide it to their mouth, satisfying their desire to eat independently. Introduce the concept of pinching, using your pointer finger and thumb to grasp items, as early as 2–3 months by providing your baby with appropriate or safe toys or objects (such as a pacifier) to practice handling. As they get older, continue to take advantage of opportunities for them to grasp and pinch as you navigate day by day. Here are just a few activities that specifically focus on fine motor skills; there are several more throughout the activities in chapters 5 and 6.

#24 **Activity**: Stringing Beads

Age Group: 3+

Materials Needed: String or yarn, beads, scissors

What to Do: Cut pieces of the string or yarn and tie a knot towards one end that is big enough to keep the beads from falling off. Push the string through the holes in the beads one by one, leaving enough room to tie a second knot towards the other end of the string.

#25 **Activity**: Puzzles with Knobs

Age Group: 2+

Materials Needed: Any puzzles that have knobs on the pieces

What to Do: Present your toddler with the puzzle and take the pieces out so they can pick them up by the knobs and work them back into their proper place.

#26 **Activity**: Domino Line Up

Age Group: 3+

Materials Needed: Dominoes

What to Do: Choose an area (hard flooring is best) with enough space for your child to line up the dominoes standing on their sides in any shape they desire. Most children will enjoy knocking the dominoes down as well. This is a great activity to work on those fine motor skills as they try to protect the dominoes they've already lined up until it's time to knock them down.

#27 **Activity**: Wrap Around

Age Group: 2.5+

Materials Needed: A hot glue gun, a 12-inch-long wooden dowel rod, 16–17-inch-long string that has some elastic on the inside, a fine-tip sharpie, and a knife.

What to Do: Very carefully rock the knife back and forth on the top of the dowel rod until a groove is started, and then move back and forth to create a slit—do not apply too much pressure, or the dowel rod will split too much. Do the same thing on the bottom of the dowel rod. Put a dab of hot glue on the top slit, and slide one end of the string into the slit with the hot glue. Once completely dry, wrap the string around and around the rod like a candy cane until you reach the bottom and slide it into the slit. Take the sharpie and follow the path of the string, marking all the way down the rod. Unwind the string. Present it to your child for them to wind around, following the markings on the rod, until they reach the end and secure it into the slit. String with some elasticity holds its form better around the rod and will not slip as much as normal string.

#28 **Activity**: Q-Tips and Tweezers

Age Group: 3+

Materials Needed: A few Q-tips, a pair of tweezers, and a small container

What to Do: Put a small pile of Q-tips in front of your toddler and equip them with a pair of tweezers so they can pick one Q-tip up at a time and place it in the container.

COGNITIVE DEVELOPMENT + ACTIVITIES

Cognitive development is happening in your child, regardless of what they are doing. Therefore, the quality of what your child engages in matters and has an effect on their cognitive development. Montessori philosophy aims to capitalize on the toddler years, when an incredible amount of brain development is occurring so that a solid foundation for logic, mathematics, problem-solving, and more is laid for your child to build upon as they age. Activities that promote number recognition, counting, or matching numbers with quantities will spark mathematical development and tie together with problem-solving as the activities are set up to follow a logical pattern.

These are some materials you may find in most Montessori classrooms or that you can purchase or build for your home:

- **Peg Number Board**: Ten flat pieces of wood, each labeled 1–10, have the appropriate number of holes in them to accommodate pegs being inserted to match the number.
- **Number Rods**: Ten rods of wood, all the same width but increasing in size, that alternate in color.
- **Sandpaper Letter and Numbers**: Cards that have the alphabet and numbers on them can be traced with sandpaper so the child can trace them with their finger to begin learning the shape for writing and general recognition.
- **Math Beads**: A set of 10 beaded strings, the first with a single bead, the second with two beads, all the way up to 10. The child can set them out or hang them on hooks in the proper order.

Below are a few cognitive development-specific activities you can try, and there will be more in Chapters 5 and 6.

#29 **Activity**: More Drops

Age Group: 3+

Materials Needed: Ten index cards, a marker, ten clear cups or water bottles, one color of food coloring, water, and a spoon or stick for stirring.

What to Do: Label the index cards 1 to 10. Fill each cup halfway with water and line them up side by side with the labels 1 to 10 in front of them. Your child will put one drop of food coloring into the first cup, two in the second, and so on until there are ten in the tenth. Stir each cup with a spoon if needed. They can observe the progression of the cups getting darker in color based on the growing number of drops.

#30 **Activity**: Matching Block Layouts

Age Group: 3+

Materials Needed: Wooden blocks, paper, ruler, pencil, or writing utensil

What to Do: Use the paper, ruler, and pencil to draw several flat layouts that your child will look at and attempt to match with their blocks. You can do one layout on individual index cards or several on one sheet of paper. The blocks won't be stacked on top of one another but rather in flat arrangements.

#31 **Activity**: Perfect Fit

Age Group: 3.5+

Materials Needed: Measuring cups sizes 1, 3/4, 1/2, 1/4, and 1/8 (if you own sizes 2 and 1-½, you can definitely add them to this activity; it is just more rare to have a set that includes those), 5–7 clear plastic cups (standard size), and 3–6 cups of sand.

What to Do: Use the measuring cups to scoop 1 cup of sand into the first plastic cup, 3/4 of a cup into the second, 1/2 cup into the third, 1/4 cup into the fourth, and 1/8 cup into the fifth. If using more sizes than those five, perform the same process with them. Mix around the order in which the clear cups are sitting and place the measuring cups in front of them randomly as well (do not have the correct measuring cup in front of the plastic cup it goes with). Your child will then observe the different amounts of sand in the cups as compared to the different sizes of measuring cups in front of them and pour the sand from the cup into the correct measuring cup. They'll know if they did it correctly if the measuring cup doesn't overflow and isn't lacking either.

#32 **Activity**: Drawing Number Rods

Age Group: 3.5+

Materials Needed: Paper, pencil, maker, and ruler

What to Do: Use the ruler and pencil to mark a 1 in. line near the bottom left edge of the paper upwards; move to the right and pencil a 2 in. line; move again and mark a 3 in. line until you are on the other side of the paper for a 10 in. line. At the top of each line, label them 1–10. Place the paper and a marker in front of your child so they can trace over the lines and numbers you drew with the pencil. You can also cut two different colors of duct tape into thin strips taped to themselves and cut them into 1 in., 3 in., 5 in., 7 in., and 9 in. with one color and 2 in., 4 in., 6 in., 8 in., and 10 in. with the other color, and your child can line them up on the correct spot on the paper.

#33 **Activity**: Tetris Blocks

Age Group: 3+

Materials Needed: Tetris blocks

What to Do: Your child will manipulate the blocks to fit nicely without any gaps and can accomplish this in several different ways many times over.

"Sharing knowledge is like lighting a candle from another's flame."

THOMAS JEFFERSON

Helping others, especially parents seeking guidance, is a rewarding journey. So, I've got a question for you...

Would you share insights that could guide another parent, even if no one knew it was you?

This person, they're a lot like you or how you once were—eager to learn, seeking support, and unsure where to start.

Our aim is to make the Montessori philosophy accessible to everyone. Everything I do revolves around that aim. And, the key to achieving it is reaching as many people as possible.

Here's where your help matters. Most folks tend to judge a book by its reviews, and that's where you come in, championing for a fellow parent you've never met:

Could you support that fellow parent by leaving a review for this book?

Your gesture costs nothing but a minute of your time, yet it could alter the course of another parent's life. Your review might:

- ...help a family establish a nurturing environment.
- ...guide a parent towards nurturing independence.

- ...assist someone in fostering their child's love for learning.
- ...support a caregiver in navigating the toddler years with ease.
- ...inspire one more family to create beautiful memories during toddlerhood.

Leave a review by scanning the QR code below:

With heartfelt gratitude,
Your ally, Amy Lee Terres

PART THREE
APPLICATION

CHAPTER 5
INDOOR ACTIVITIES

> *The exercises, which children do, help their adaptation to the environment. The first adaptation to the environment is to become conscious of it. To become conscious, they need to acquire knowledge. Children acquire knowledge through experience in the environment.*
>
> MARIA MONTESSORI

Many of the following activities can be tinkered with to become more advanced for older children or more simple for younger children. Let your creative juices flow, and think about ways to incorporate colors, counting, spelling, and more into activities that might not specifically focus on those things. In general, the creation of the activity through the listed materials will either be done by you as the adult, but if there is anything you think your child would be able to do for themselves or assist you with, then bring them into that part of the activity as well. Several of the activities have overlapping materials that can be used many times for a variety of other listed activities; this was intentional so as to make things more cost-effective and save time. Remember to take lots of pictures and cherish this precious time of heightened exploration with your toddler.

LIVING ROOM

#34 **Activity**: Lid Matching

Age Group: 2+

Materials Needed: Containers, boxes, and/or jars of any size that have lids.

What to Do: Lay out the containers with their lids removed and have your child match the lid to the correct container.

#35 **Activity**: Sand Writing

Age Group: 2.5+

Materials Needed: Shallow container, sand, index cards, and a marker.

What to Do: Use a marker to write out each letter of the alphabet and the numbers 0–9 on individual index cards. Cover the bottom of the container with a layer of sand. Place an index card above the container so your child can practice writing what is on the card with their finger in the sand. An alternative to sand could be salt.

#36 **Activity**: Secret Agents

Age Group: 3.5+

Materials Needed: Tape, red yarn (or any color), and a hallway. A hallway would work best, but if you do not have a hallway, you can create a narrower space using available furniture.

What to Do: Use the tape and yarn to create "lasers" that are shooting in various directions and heights from wall to wall. Your child will attempt to weave through the laser maze like a secret agent to get to the other side untouched.

#37 **Activity**: Is it Magnetic?

Age Group: 4+

Materials Needed: Three small, shallow containers, various nonmagnetic items such as a rock, a small wooden or plastic toy, a pencil, a hair bow, etc., and various magnetic items such as a paperclip, key, binder clip, magna-tile, tweezers, etc.

What to Do: Place all the items in one of the containers. Designate one of the empty containers as magnetic and the other as nonmagnetic. Your child will separate the items into the proper containers.

#38 **Activity**: Create a Track

Age Group: 3+

Materials Needed: Painters tape, toy car(s).

What to Do: Put down the painters tape along the ground wherever the child wants (and is allowed) for it to go. Drive the toy car from one end to the other.

#39 **Activity**: Obstacle Course

Age Group: 2.5+

Materials Needed: Miscellaneous items around the living room or house, i.e., pillows, chairs, small furniture, etc.

What to Do: Move items around to create a unique obstacle course that involves weaving around objects, crawling under chairs, jumping over pillows, etc. You can also use painters tape on the floor to create obstacles, such as a straight line where the child must walk with one foot directly in front of the other, an X where the child stops to jump up and down five times, etc.

#40 **Activity**: Shoo Fly!

Age Group: 3+

Materials Needed: Fly swatter; prints of pictures of various insects, ensuring that a few of them are flies.

What to Do: Have your child hold the fly swatter and flip your prints over one by one. Your child will use the fly swatter to hit the picture when they see a fly.

#41 **Activity**: Hide-and-Seek

Age Group: 9 months+

Materials Needed: None

What to Do: Once your baby is crawling proficiently, start introducing hide-and-seek to work on your baby's problem-solving skills. Let them watch you disappear behind a piece of furniture so they can come and find you. As your child ages, this can turn into a full-on hide-and-seek game with your child on the hiding or seeking end.

#42 **Activity**: Inside or Outside?

Age Group: 3+

Materials Needed: Three small containers, a collection of outdoor items such as a rock, flower, stick, pinecone, leaf, etc., and a collection of indoor items such as a notepad, measuring cup, sock, tube of toothpaste, etc.

What to Do: Place all items together in one of the containers, labeling one of the empty containers "indoor" and the other "outdoor." Your child will separate the items based on where they belong.

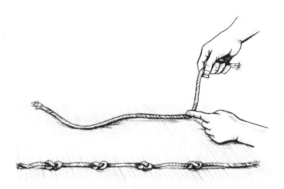

#43 **Activity**: Tying Knots

Age Group: 4+

Materials Needed: Two thin pieces of rope about 1.5 feet long each.

What to Do: Tie four knots equal distance apart from one another along one of the strings; this will be the example your child will be looking at as they attempt to match it with the second piece of rope that has no knots in it.

#44 **Activity**: Smelling Candles

Age Group: 2.5+

Materials Needed: Variety of candles

What to Do: If you're anything like me, there's a shelf some-where in your house that has a few candles on it waiting until it's their turn to be used. Pull these out and sit with your child so they can smell them. Discuss the differences between them. Is it sweet? Is it outdoorsy? Fresh and clean?

#45 **Activity**: Build a Fort

Age Group: 3+

Materials Needed: Blankets, pillows, sleeping bags, and various furniture.

What to Do: You know this symbol "☺" Gather all the supplies and create a masterpiece. Don't forget special touches such as books and a flashlight.

BEDROOM

#46 **Activity**: Emotion Recognition

Age Group: 2.5+

Materials Needed: Paper and markers to make labels. Prints of people expressing various emotions: happiness, sadness, anger, confusion, fear, disgust, surprise, etc. *Bonus:* Reach out to family members and assign them an emotion to be able to use their photos instead of ones of strangers or that are animated. This will allow for familiarity with those family members to grow, especially if they live far away.

What to Do: Lay out the pictures in front of your child and have them label the photos with the correct emotion. You can also use this time to discuss the reasons why we might feel one of these emotions and what we can do to overcome the negative ones. Discuss that emotions are not bad but that we should work to take control of our emotions rather than letting them control us.

#47 **Activity**: Color Match Up

Age Group: 2+

Materials Needed: Different sheets of colored paper: red, blue, yellow, green, orange, purple, pink, black, white, brown, gray, etc. Various toys or objects from around the room.

What to Do: Lay out the pieces of colored paper (as many or as few as you choose); your child can grab items from around the room that match the color of the paper and place them accordingly.

#48 **Activity**: Pairing Shoes

Age Group: 2+

Materials Needed: Shoes

What to Do: Take one shoe from each pair and move it to a different location from its partner shoe. Your child can take one shoe at a time and place it back with its correct partner.

#49 **Activity**: Pay For Clothes

Age Group: 3+

Materials Needed: Pennies, nickels, dimes, quarters, dollars, paper or index cards, markers, tape, a cup, and a medium-sized container.

What to Do: Use the index cards and marker to write how much a part of the child's outfit for the day will cost, i.e., five pennies for their socks, 10 dimes for their shoes, five nickels and two quarters for their pants, seven dollars for their shirt, etc. Tape/secure the amount to each item and provide a container with plenty of change and dollars. Have your child place their payment for one of the items in a cup and present it to you to check; if it's correct, they can obtain the item and move on to the next one. As your child increases in age, you can advance this activity by labeling the clothing as $1.75 or 50¢, so they have to calculate and understand the worth of each coin or dollar instead of counting out the coins that you've specified.

#50 **Activity**: Blanket Shapes

Age Group: 3.5+

Materials Needed: One blanket

What to Do: Have your child spread the blanket out on the floor and identify its shape. If it's a rectangle, they can try to make a fold that will turn it into a square; from there, they can make another fold to turn it into a triangle. Each time a new shape is created, they can count the sides of the shape; if you want it to include more movement, they can jump along each of the sides as they count or try to jump from corner to corner.

#51 **Activity**: Organize Stuffed Animals

Age Group: 2.5+

Materials Needed: Stuffed Animals

What to Do: Designate an area of the bedroom or bed where the stuffed animals are supposed to be. If your child plays with them, ensure that they take the time to organize them back into an orderly fashion. While playing with the stuffed animals, they can also line them up from biggest to smallest or place them in groups based on their kind.

#52 **Activity**: Scarf Tying

Age Group: 3+

Materials Needed: A child-sized scarf

What to Do: Your child can practice tying a basic knot using a scarf that they wrap around their back so that both ends are in front of them, and then tie a knot on their belly.

BATHROOM

#53 **Activity**: Matching Game

Age Group: 2+

Materials Needed: Toothbrush, toothpaste, hairbrush, comb, other bathroom basics, paper, a pen or marker, and a shallow container.

What to Do: Collect the items, place them on the paper, and trace them. Place the items in a shallow bin in front of your child with the paper; they will match the item to the correct shape on the paper.

#54 **Activity**: Fizzy Bath Mixture

Age Group: 3.5+

Materials Needed: Medium bowl, small bowl, mixing spoon, 1/2 cup baking soda, 1/2 cup citric acid, 1/4 cup Epsom salt, 1/8 cup cornstarch, 1 tablespoon melted coconut oil, 1/2 table-spoon water, 4–5 drops of essential oil, and 4–5 drops of food coloring.

What to Do: In a medium bowl, mix baking soda, citric acid, Epsom salt, and cornstarch. In a small bowl, mix coconut oil, water, essential oils, and food coloring. Very slowly, pour the wet mixture into the dry mixture while stirring. Once combined, it is ready to be used and put into the bathtub for bath time. If you let it sit a little bit until it is ready to be put in the bathtub, it will harden up a little like a bath bomb, which is perfectly fine.

#55 **Activity**: Squeaky Clean

Age Group: 3+

Materials Needed: Paper towels and glass cleaner

What to Do: Guide your child to spray the mirror and then wipe it dry with the paper towel. They can be involved in cleaning any other areas as well, such as wiping the countertops.

#56 **Activity**: Bathtub Alphabet

Age Group: 3+

Materials Needed: Alphabet letters for the bathtub

What to Do: Talk about the letters of the alphabet and practice the sounds they make during bathtime. Start showing your child how the letters and the sounds they make connect to make words that we can read. Line them up along the edge of the tub to show cat, dog, sit, tub, bath, water, and other simple words.

#57 **Activity**: Spray Bottle

Age Group: 2.5+

Materials Needed: Small spray bottle

What to Do: Fill the bottle with water or some sort of cleaner. Allow your child to practice using a spray bottle by spraying the shower or bathtub walls. This activity does not have to be isolated to the bathroom; it could be on the kitchen counter-tops or even outside on the concrete, anywhere you deem appropriate for your child to work on this skill.

PLAYROOM

#58 **Activity**: Create Your Own Board Game

Age Group: 4+

Materials Needed: Paper, scissors, markers, cardboard box, ruler, tracing tools, and any miscellaneous items of your choosing.

What to Do: Supply your child with several materials and let them come up with their own board games with rules and how to win. Then, play it together and see if it works. This activity majorly promotes creative thinking!

#59 **Activity**: What Day Is It?

Age Group: 3+

Materials Needed: Paper, markers, scissors, and three small to medium containers.

What to Do: Create seven strips of paper labeled Sunday, Monday, etc. Create 31 squares labeled 1, 2, 3,... 31. Create 12 strips labeled January, February, etc. Your child can be a part of the creation of these if you so desire. Use three shallow bins to house the days of the week, numbers, and months. Set them up in a designated spot where they will be safe throughout your day-to-day activities. Each day, your child can pull out the appropriate day of the week and date within the month to keep track and learn the order of the days and months. This activity can be beefed up by using numbered blocks instead of paper strips or by purchasing or creating something with more finality than this paper option. The paper option can also be laminated to make it more sturdy.

#60 **Activity**: Follow the Line

Age Group: 3.5+

Materials Needed: Yarn or string, push pins, a piece of cardboard or a foam board, scissors, a sharpie, or a marker.

What to Do: Use the sharpie to draw a few different lines from one end of the board to the other, and use the push pins on any "turns" along the line where it changes direction. Use the scissors to make a cut on the edge of the board where the lines you have drawn come to an end. Cut pieces of string that are long enough to cover the span of the line and have extra to hang off the edge. Make sure there is a push pin inserted at the start of the line, and tie the yarn to the push pin. From there, your child will take the yarn and navigate it to match the line, wrapping it around the push pins as they go to secure it. Once they reach the end, they can secure the rest of the yarn by sliding it into the slit that was made on the side of the board.

#61 **Activity**: Musical Instruments

Age Group: 2+

Materials Needed: Toy instruments or create your own instruments with other household materials, i.e., upside-down pots with two wooden spoons for drumming.

What to Do: If possible, have a set of toys or children's musical instruments such as a tambourine, piano, xylophone, guitar, etc. There are many options for color-neutral, wooden instrument sets that you can find. Have designated times for your child to explore these instruments. If you have multiple children, they can work together to create a band and put on a performance.

#62 **Activity**: Homemade Maracas

Age Group: 2+

Materials Needed: Two plastic Easter eggs, duct tape, four plastic spoons, and rice or dry beans

What to Do: Open the Easter eggs and fill them halfway with rice or dry beans. Close and secure the seam with a strip of duct tape. Place two plastic spoons on each side of one of the Easter eggs, with the curves matching, and secure them with another strip or two of duct tape. Hold the handles of the spoons together and secure them with a strip of duct tape. Repeat with the other egg and spoons. Give it to your child to shake! For children a little older, they can be a part of the maraca-making process.

#63 **Activity**: Animals that Jump

Age Group: 2.5+

Materials Needed: Print cards with pictures of a variety of animals, being sure to include a few kangaroos, rabbits, frogs, dolphins, or any other animals known for jumping.

What to Do: Your child will stand in front of you, and you'll flip over one card at a time. When they recognize an animal that jumps, they will jump. This activity can be expanded by having them move in whatever way any of the animals on the cards typically move, such as getting on all fours for a dog or lion or wiggling on the ground for a snake.

#64 **Activity**: Stacking Blocks

Age Group: 2+

Materials Needed: Wooden blocks of any kind/size

What to Do: Your child can stack blocks on top of one another, attempting to get it as tall as possible without falling down. They can make single-column towers or multiple towers grouped closely together for more strength.

#65 **Activity**: Cover and Find

Age Group: 1+

Materials Needed: One to three cups and an object small enough to fit underneath the cup.

What to Do: For the youngest ones, show them you are covering up an object with the cup and allow them to remove the cup so they can find it. As your child gets older, you can begin using two or three cups, covering up an object with one of them, moving them around, and seeing if your child can track and successfully uncover the object.

#66 **Activity**: Can You Reach It?

Age Group: 18 months+

Materials Needed: An empty container that once held yogurt, sour cream, or something of the like that is of a similar size, scissors or a knife, painters tape or duct tape, a few cotton balls, and a few Q-tips.

What to Do: Remove the lid from the empty and clean container and cut a hole that is slightly smaller than the width of a cotton ball. If necessary, use the tape to add protection around the hole that you cut in case there are any pokey spots. Return the lid to the container and place it in front of your child with the cotton balls and Q-tips. They can drop them into the container and work on getting them back out.

#67 **Activity**: Body Parts

Age Group: 4+

Materials Needed: A large piece of paper or roll of paper, writing or coloring utensils, index cards, and glue.

What to Do: Label the index cards with as many body parts as you want, such as arm, leg, thigh, ankle, toes, head, nose, shoulder, etc. Roll paper out onto the floor big enough for your child to lay down on their back on it. Trace the outline of their body with a writing utensil. Have them glue the labels in the correct place on the outline of their body. If they are exploring writing, they can write the body parts onto the paper instead of using pre-made labels.

#68 **Activity**: Bodily Organs

Age Group: 4

Materials Needed: A large piece of paper or roll of paper; writing or coloring utensils; glue; printouts of various animated organs in the body, i.e., the heart, lungs, kidney, stomach, intestines, bladder, liver, etc.

What to Do: Roll paper out onto the floor big enough for your child to lay down on their back on it. Trace the outline of their body with a writing utensil. Provide them with printouts of the pictures of the organs and discuss where they go so your child can glue them in the correct area of the body. If you do not have the printouts, you can still do this activity with your child, who can draw or write the names of the organs onto the paper to the best of their ability.

#69 **Activity**: Playdough Sculpting

Age Group: 2+

Materials Needed: Playdough and a clean surface. *Optional:* playdough cutters

What to Do: Situate your child in a space to make playdough creations. They can use playdough cookie cutters to aid in their experimentation.

KITCHEN

#70 **Activity**: Rinsing Fruits and Veggies

Age Group: 2+

Materials Needed: Step stool, strainer, sink, fruit, and/or vegetables.

What to Do: Allow your child to have a good reach into the sink to grab pieces of fruit or vegetables to rinse under a stream of water and set in a strainer.

#71 **Activity**: Liquid Transfer

Age Group: 2+

Materials Needed: Two large bowls or containers, water, a measuring cup, and potentially a towel.

What to Do: Fill one of the bowls with water, place the second bowl a few inches away, and provide your child with the measuring cup so they can scoop water out of the full bowl and dump it into the empty bowl. This can be done over the sink or on the floor with a towel underneath.

#72 **Activity**: Sweeping Messes

Age Group: 2+

Materials Needed: Small broom and dustpan

What to Do: Make a mess on the floor to be swept up, or use pre-existing messes as a chance to involve your child in the clean-up process.

#73 **Activity**: Funnel Fun

Age Group: 3+

Materials Needed: Funnel, two cups, medium container, and any liquid.

What to Do: Fill the medium container with water. You can add a drop of food coloring to appeal to the senses a little more if desired. Place your child at the sink or outside if it is a nice day. They will use one cup to scoop water and pour it into the funnel that is being held over the second cup with their other hand.

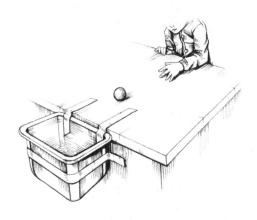

#74 **Activity**: Roll Ball to Bucket

Age Group: 2+

Materials Needed: Painters tape or duct tape; a small bucket or container; a table or countertop; a round ball or balls.

What to Do: Tape or somehow secure the bucket to the edge of a table with the opening upwards and in line with the edge. Position your child on the opposite end of the table with the balls so they can attempt to roll the ball across the table to land in the bucket.

#75 **Activity**: Make Popsicles

Age Group: 2.5+

Materials Needed: Popsicle sticks and a popsicle mold (some come with sticks already). If you don't own a mold and want to try and use what you already have on hand, alternatives could be shot glasses, ice cube trays (mini-pops), muffin pans, or empty individual yogurt containers.

What to Do: Yogurt is a good base for creamier popsicles, but any pureed fruit or veggie with or without yogurt can be put into the popsicle mold and sweetened with honey (for 12+ months only) or sugar. There are many recipes out there if you don't want to experiment on your own. Whatever you decide, have your toddler help prepare the mixture, pour it into the mold, secure the popsicle sticks, and place it in the freezer.

#76 **Activity**: Help Prepare Soup

Age Group: 3+

Materials Needed: Measuring cup, water, and pot to be used for soup

What to Do: Place your child on their step stool at the kitchen sink with a measuring cup and the empty pot on the counter next to the sink. Tell your child how many cups of water are needed for the recipe so they can fill the measuring cup and dump it into the pot. If some sort of broth is needed for the soup, they can hold their measuring cup over the pot while you pour the broth into the cup, and then they tip it into the pot.

#77 **Activity**: Wash a Pot

Age Group: 3+

Materials Needed: Sponge, dish soap, and a dirty pot

What to Do: Since pots are big and wide, they are great practice for your child to learn to wash dishes. The pot doesn't *have* to be dirty; washing an already clean pot won't cause any harm. Set up your child at the kitchen sink on a stool so that they can reach it. Allow them to wet the sponge, put dish soap on it, and create a lather in the pot so they can scrub it all over. Then turn the water back on so they can rinse it off.

#78 **Activity**: Count your Snack

Age Group: 3+

Materials Needed: Ten clear plastic cups or small plastic bowls; a medium bowl or container; ten index cards; a marker or sharpie; and a snack item that can be counted out, such as goldfish.

What to Do: Label the index cards with the numbers 1–10 and set them in front of each clear cup or bowl that is placed in a line. Pour your child's snack into a medium bowl. They can use their fingers or a spoon to put one goldfish in the first bowl labeled "1" and two in the second that is labeled "2," and so on and so forth until they have ten in the tenth one.

#79 **Activity**: Hot and Cold

Age Group: 2+

Materials Needed: Ice pack and a heat pack

What to Do: Set the ice pack and the heat pack in front of your child and let them explore the difference in sensation between the temperatures.

#80 **Activity**: Drops of Color

Age Group: 3+

Materials Needed: A few empty plastic water bottles, water, and food coloring.

What to Do: Your child can fill the water bottles with water and line them up on a table or the counter. They can put a few drops of food coloring in it and watch it change colors. If you only buy primary colors for food coloring, you can discuss mixing yellow and blue to create green or blue and red to create purple.

#81 **Activity**: Using a Rolling Pin

Age Group: 3+

Materials Needed: A rolling pin and any recipe requiring the use of one.

What to Do: For any recipe for cookies, bread, etc., that requires flattened dough, set your child up on a stool to reach the counter and allow them to use the rolling pin.

LAUNDRY ROOM

#82 **Activity**: Homemade Laundry Detergent

Age Group: 4+

Materials Needed: Large plastic storage container, wooden spoon, blender, half of a box of baking soda, one box of borax powder, one container of OxiClean, and two boxes of fels-naptha flakes (it is sometimes difficult to find the flakes option; if you cannot find it, then get two of the bars instead, and note you will also need a grater). Optional: One or two containers of fragrance crystals or fragrance boosters.

What to Do: If using fels-naptha bars: Use a grater to grate the bars all the way down and then place them into the blender. If using fels-naptha flakes, pour them into the blender and blend them into a finer powder. Pour all ingredients into the storage container, mix thoroughly with a wooden spoon, and pour the detergent into whatever storage container(s) you plan to keep it in. Use 1–2 tablespoons per load.

#83 **Activity**: Sponge Clean

Age Group: 3+

Materials Needed: Sponge or a Mr. Clean Magic Eraser

What to Do: Free cleaning! Wet and wring out the sponge or magic eraser for your child to wipe baseboards, floors, doors, etc. Most surfaces should be fine for them to scrub, but take caution on the walls in case the paint might rub off depending on the age of the home and the quality of the paint.

#84 **Activity**: Ironing Practice

Age Group: 3+

Materials Needed: Mini ironing board, mini-iron, and a shirt or towel

What to Do: Your child can use the turned OFF (don't even plug it in) iron to practice ironing a towel or shirt on the ironing board. They can perhaps do this nearby while you do some actual ironing. Once they are a little older and you feel they are ready, you can guide them with the iron on low heat. Your diligent supervision is a MUST during this activity.

#85 **Activity**: Start The Laundry

Age Group: 3+

Materials Needed: Step stool, laundry detergent, washing machine, dirty laundry (you don't have to search hard for this one, I'm sure).

What to Do: Bring a step stool up to the washing machine so your toddler can drop the clothes inside. Have them scoop powdered detergent or pour liquid detergent into the designated spot on the washing machine, close the lid, and press the buttons to start the cycle.

#86 **Activity**: What is Laundry?

Age Group: 3+

Materials Needed: A laundry basket, a piece of paper wider and longer than the laundry basket, and crayons or colored pencils.

What to Do: Place paper on the ground with the laundry basket face down on top of it. Your toddler can take a crayon or colored pencil and trace around the edge of the basket. Remove the basket and place your child on the floor with the paper and coloring materials while you are nearby, folding laundry. Your child can attempt to draw what kinds of things go in the laundry basket while you fold. They can observe the types of clothes you are handling to inspire them to draw shirts, pants, towels, socks, etc. They can also try to use the correct color for the piece of clothing they saw you handle.

#87 **Activity**: Help Put Laundry Away

Age Group: 2.5+

Materials Needed: Folded Laundry

What to Do: Hand a pile of folded laundry to your child and have them put it where it belongs, then move on to the next type of clothing. This will work on their coordination by trying to keep the clothes neatly folded while putting them away.

OFFICE OR STUDY

#88 **Activity**: Organize Writing Utensils

Age Group: 3+

Materials Needed: Any drawer, container, or space in your home that has pens or markers. One to two sheets of plain paper.

What to Do: It may be necessary to aid in collecting the pens and markers that are going to be tested for younger children and then set them up in a controlled environment. For those a little older, the activity could start off with a "hunt" to collect the pens and markers and bring them to a designated area. Once pens, markers, paper, and child(ren) are settled at a table or on the floor, have them test each pen and marker one by one to see if it still has ink and functions as it should. Your child can organize them into a "trash" pile and a "good" pile. One step further would be to organize the "good" pile according to their kind and/or color.

#89 **Activity**: Write Then Mail A Card

Age Group: 2.5+

Materials Needed: Card, envelope, pencil or pen, postage stamp

What to Do: Depending on age and writing abilities, your toddler can draw and/or write a card to a friend, grandparent, or another family member and learn about how the postal system works. You can take a trip to the post office to send the card or take a walk to the mailbox.

#90 **Activity**: Stamps

Age Group: 2.5+

Materials Needed: Stamps and paper.

What to Do: Use the stamps on the paper; if they are skin-friendly stamps, you may allow them to put some on their hands, arms, or body. This is good for stimulating your child's proprioceptive sense as they figure out how much pressure they need to use when pushing down on the stamps.

#91 **Activity**: Stickers

Age Group: 2.5+

Materials Needed: Any stickers, paper, or a safe place to stick them.

What to Do: This can be done more as a free play where your child puts stickers on the paper wherever or however they please, or you can have a variety of sizes and shapes for the stickers and trace them on a separate piece of paper ahead of time so your child can match them to the correct space.

#92 **Activity**: Create a Zoo

Age Group: 3+

Materials Needed: Wildlife magazine(s), scissors, paper, glue, or tape

What to Do: Your toddler can flip through the magazine and use the scissors to cut out images of animals that they find and then glue or tape them on a piece of paper to create their own personal zoo.

#93 **Activity**: Human Shredder

Age Group: 6+ months

Materials Needed: Paper that you do not need or care about

What to Do: For babies: Hand them some paper, let them throw it around, rip it, taste it, and destroy it. For toddlers: Make it the goal for them to use two hands to rip and tear it up to their heart's content.

#94 **Activity**: Personal Planets

Age Group: 3.5+

Materials Needed: Battery-powered tea lights, white ping pong balls, a knife or scissors, paint, and a cardboard lid at least 2 inches deep.

What to Do: Use a knife to cut a hole in the ping pong ball that is big enough to be pushed over the "flame" of the tea light and still fit snuggly. Squeeze a couple lines of paint per color along the bottom of the cardboard lid, set a ping pong ball inside the lid, and hand it to your child to tilt the lid from side to side, back and forth, so the ping pong ball rolls around and gets covered with paint. Remove the ping pong ball and set it in a safe place to dry. Once it is dry, push it onto the tea light and turn it on to view your child's personal planet.

#95 **Activity**: Build a Robot

Age Group: 3.5+

Materials Needed: Large cardboard box, scissors, markers and/or paint, and packing tape.

What to Do: Your child will turn the box upside down and cut off the flaps. Cut a hole in the bottom of the box for their head to fit through and a hole on the left and right sides of the box for each of their arms to fit through. Use packing tape to secure the bottom of the box closed after the hole for their head is cut, if needed. Your child can use markers or paint to decorate all sides of the box to look like a robot with gears, screws, or whatever they desire. Once it's dry, they can wear it and pretend to be robots.

INDOOR GYM OR EXERCISE AREA

#96 **Activity**: Belly Breathing

Age Group: 3+

Materials Needed: None

What to Do: Sit cross-legged on the floor or in any comfortable area. Have your child place their hands gently over their belly and take a slow, deep breath, trying to make their belly stick out and "fill up with air." If they are old enough, you can have them place one hand over their chest instead and compare filling their chest with air versus their belly, and talk about how when we fill our chest with air, this is more shallow breathing, but good deep breaths will fill and expand our belly area and ensure that we are getting good oxygen. Have them count in their heads as they breathe in and out, attempting to have a slow intake and release.

#97 **Activity**: Yoga

Age Group: 3+

Materials Needed: Yoga mats and access to YouTube if you want to utilize online videos

What to Do: Set up yoga mats in an open space; play a YouTube video or other content to follow along with a kid-friendly yoga session. There are many resources out there that are tailored just for kids. If you have enough knowledge of yoga, feel free to lead your kids in various stretches and breathing exercises.

#98 **Activity**: Dancing

Age Group: 1+

Materials Needed: A way to play music

What to Do: Play music and dance around with your child!

#99 **Activity**: Faster, Slower

Age Group: 3+

Materials Needed: A way to play music

What to Do: You can do this activity with jumping jacks or running. Start playing music at a normal volume and have your child either do jumping jacks or run laps. Increase the volume for them to increase their speed; lower the volume for them to slow down. When the music gets very low, they will be pushing the limits of their gross motor skills by attempting to control their body in a "slow motion" fashion with a movement that is typically done more quickly.

#100 **Activity**: Up and Down

Age Group: 3+

Materials Needed: None

What to Do: Your child lays flat on their back until you (or someone) says, "Up!" They then pop as fast as they can, stretch their fingers to the sky, and stand on their tippy toes to reach as tall as they can until they head, "Down!" Then they relax down to the ground, flat on their backs, and so on and so forth.

CHAPTER 6
OUTDOOR ACTIVITIES

> *All animals and vegetables, superior animals, inferior animals, insects, etc., have a cosmic task. All are agents, maintainers, and conservers of this order in the environment.*

MARIA MONTESSORI

The end of Chapter 7 discusses more details about the power of nature, but I want to emphasize here before you dive into the activities that any way you increase the amount of time your children spend outside is highly encouraged. Even sitting on the porch/balcony/deck to eat meals in the fresh air is impactful. If you have a covered area outside your home, many of the indoor activities can be moved outside too. Let your kids run, play, and get dirty. Let them experience water, mountains, beaches, and forests. The outdoors can shape and mold us in many ways; let's be diligent about exposing our children to it as much as possible.

FAIR WEATHER

#101 **Activity**: Melting Ice + Counting Practice

Age Group: 2+

Materials Needed: Ice cubes, a bucket or container, a sunny area, and preferably a portion of concrete for better visibility.

What to Do: Take a bucket of ice cubes outside into the sun, have your child remove one cube at a time, and place it in the sun to melt. If applicable, children can count how many seconds it takes to melt. If you are able to find an area that has shade and sun close together, you can have your child compare the amount of time it takes an ice cube to melt in the sun versus the shade. *Bonus:* Your child can keep a log over time that documents the outdoor temperature and average time of the ice cubes melting to increase their awareness that hotter temperatures = faster melting process.

#102 **Activity**: Planting Seeds

Age Group: 3+

Materials Needed: Seeds of your choosing, a place to plant them, a spade, and water.

What to Do: This activity will look different depending on whether you live in an apartment, on a farm, or somewhere in between. Your child can dig a hole, place the seed in the ground, cover it, and water it. If you do not have a place in the ground, you can use a flowerpot, buy or collect dirt, plant seeds in the pot, and water. If you live in a place that has enough yard to have a garden, even just one raised bed, utilize that space so your child can cultivate their love for nature and increase their understanding about where food comes from and the way the earth provides for our needs.

#103 **Activity**: Potting Plants

Age Group: 3+

Materials Needed: Flowerpots of any kind, including window boxes or balcony boxes; a few plants from a nursery; extra dirt; and water.

What to Do: Fill flowerpots/boxes with enough dirt, place a plant in a pot and finish covering it with dirt, then water, and place in an appropriate place to get the recommended amount of sunlight depending on the type of plants or flowers purchased.

#104 **Activity**: Watering Plants

Age Group: 2+

Materials Needed: A watering can or water hose and plants or a garden.

What to Do: Encourage your child to take part in the everyday task of watering the plants you have inside and outside your home. Especially if they have planted seeds or potted plants, keep them engaged with the process of growth by nurturing their seedlings and fragile plants everyday.

#105 **Activity**: Rock Collecting and Grouping

Age Group: 3+

Materials Needed: None

What to Do: Your child will collect as many rocks as they please and bring them to a designated spot. They will then group them together by size. If desired, you can use clear plastic cups or small containers for them to separate the groups; otherwise, just have the groupings spread out in different piles around where they are sitting.

#106 **Activity**: Painting With Water

Age Group: 2+

Materials Needed: Paintbrushes, water, medium-to-large container

What to Do: Find a concrete surface and let your child dip paint brushes into the container filled with water and paint on the ground. They can experiment with how much faster their drawings disappear in a sunny area versus a shady area.

#107 **Activity**: Collecting Flowers and Leaves

Age Group: 2.5+

Materials Needed: Mason jars or any clear containers

What to Do: Explore an area where your child can collect leaves, flowers, or other plants and collect them into jars. If you don't have any containers, this can be a material-less activity as well, and your child can make different piles of their discoveries.

#108 **Activity**: Count Passing Vehicles

Age Group: 3+

Materials Needed: None

What to Do: Find a place to sit a safe distance from a roadway, preferably a street with a moderate amount of activity. Count with your child or have your child count the number of cars passing by. This is modifiable in several ways: count cars of a certain color; count cars of a certain type (i.e., pickup trucks); and count how many seconds go by between cars.

#109 **Activity**: How Long Is It?

Age Group: 3+

Materials Needed: Measuring Tape

What to Do: Give your child a measuring tape and show them how it works. Let them explore inside or outside, measuring anything they want. If they are old enough to write, they can keep a log of the item they measured and its length. They can compare the differences between the sizes of a centimeter, an inch, and a foot.

#110 **Activity**: Vertical Jump

Age Group: 2.5+

Materials Needed: A small bell, thin rope or thick string, a screw-eye hook

What to Do: Designate a spot outside where your child has enough room to jump and where you can secure the bell to hang down vertically from a screw-eye hook or another piece of hardware that you can utilize for your space. Hang the bell so it is just out of your child's reach when they jump vertically with their hand up. This is something you can keep outside and adjust as your child grows over the years, even into their teenage years! Increase the height of the bell once they have consistency in being able to jump and touch it with their fingers.

#111 **Activity**: Water Bucket to Empty Bucket

Age Group: 3+

Materials Needed: Two large buckets/containers, water, 5–10 medium to large toys/objects that float, and a large kid's shovel (like one for the beach).

What to Do: Fill one of the containers 3/4 with water and place the toys/objects inside. Place the empty second container several feet away from the filled one. Your child will use the shovel to scoop one of the objects up and attempt to run (or go as fast as they can) to the other bucket to deposit the object without dropping it in between. For children younger than three, you can have the buckets side by side for them to try and scoop and transfer as well. *Note:* This can also be done with a small toy shovel and smaller toys/objects that float instead of materials of a bigger size.

#112 **Activity**: Make A Bouquet

Age Group: 3+

Materials Needed: A vase, scissors

What to Do: Find a place where your child can pick flowers or greenery. Once they've collected what they want, go through the process of trimming the stems with scissors and placing the flowers in a vase with some water.

#113 **Activity**: What's In The Grass?

Age Group: 3+

Materials Needed: Magnifying glass and an outdoor area (grassy or not).

What to Do: Let your little one explore the yard with the magnifying glass and see what they discover.

#114 **Activity**: Metal Detector

Age Group: 3+

Materials Needed: A metal detector and possibly a small shovel/spade.

What to Do: Provide your child with a metal detector and let them explore the yard or a park to see what they find. If the metal detector is strong enough to detect something a little under the surface, it would be good to have a spade ready for your child to dig. *Note on this activity:* Be present with your child as they explore; they could uncover something sharp, like a screw or nail.

#115 **Activity**: Bubbles

Age Group: 6+ months

Materials Needed: Bubbles or bubble machine

What to Do: This is a tried-and-true activity that is great even for young babies who like to watch the bubbles and try to touch them, for toddlers who like to chase the bubbles, or for older kids who might be interested in making the bubble mix.

#116 **Activity**: Chalk Art

Age Group: 2.5+

Materials Needed: Chalk and an area with concrete

What to Do: Place your child on a concrete surface with chalk for drawing. As your child gets older, you can be intentional about what they attempt to draw, such as a hopscotch pad, shapes, letters, or numbers. *Tip:* We've all experienced the dreaded scratch on the knuckles or fingers when using chalk that is short and running out. To prevent this, you can put gloves on your child while they play and wash the gloves afterwards.

#117 **Activity**: Stargazing

Age Group: 2.5+

Materials Needed: None. *Optional:* Outdoor pillows, blankets, or a telescope

What to Do: Normalize looking up into the star-filled sky with your child. If you live closer to a city, be sure to take advantage of any vacations or times when you are further from the lights and pollution to point your child's gaze upwards. If you already live in a more rural area, take advantage of the clear skies on a regular basis. Lay outside with your child, try to spot shooting stars, invest in a small telescope, cozy up with blankets during the colder months, and discuss constellations and the wonder of outer space.

#118 **Activity**: Puddle Sizes

Age Group: 3.5+

Materials Needed: Water balloons, water, six paper or plastic plates, chalk, scissors, and a sharpie

What to Do: Fill 12 water balloons so that you have six matching pairs that noticeably increase in size. Using the sharpie, label the smallest two balloons with the number 1, the next size up with 2, all the way to the biggest two balloons, both labeled with a 6. One set of balloons is the control group; the other set will be popped. Find a concrete space outside and spread out the six water balloons so that when one is popped, the water will not run into the balloons next to it. Place a paper plate two feet or more above each balloon (again, you don't want the water from the balloon that will be popped to touch it), and place the control balloons on each plate with their counterparts below them sitting on the concrete. Equip your child with a pair of scissors and a stick of chalk. They will pop the balloon while it is sitting on the ground and set it aside for a few seconds until the water that comes out of it has stopped spreading. Once the water has spread, they will use the chalk to trace around the water to document the size of the spread. Repeat with all the following balloons: Your child will be able to see the difference in the size of the circles they drew around the water and how it corresponds with the balloons increasing in size. Do what you please with the control group balloons!

#119 **Activity**: Visit a Farm

Age Group: 2+

Materials Needed: None

What to Do: If you are blessed with living on acreage already, consider the many ways to be in touch with nature through farming, gardening, and potentially raising farm animals. Even just a small coop with a few chickens will entertain your children immensely. If you do not have such a space, take your child to visit a farm through a friend or relative that you know personally or through a community farm that is open to the public. The goal is to try and give your child a chance to be hands-on with the work of a farm or range.

#120 **Activity**: Go Camping

Age Group: 3+

Materials Needed: Tent, sleeping bags, weather-appropriate clothes, a battery-operated light source, a cooler with food and drinks, and any other camping gear.

What to Do: This doesn't have to be an elaborate trip to a National Park; it can simply be in your backyard if you have one! Ask a friend who has land or a bigger yard than yours if you can use a bit of space for a night. Include your child in the packing process so that they can learn how to think ahead and be prepared for what will be needed.

#121 **Activity**: Go Fishing

Age Group: 3+

Materials Needed: Fishing rods, bait, lawn chairs, a cooler with refreshments, and any other fishing gear.

What to Do: Find a pond or lake to take your child to for a fishing adventure. Remember to protect your child from the sun with appropriate clothing and hats.

RAINY WEATHER

#122 **Activity**: Collecting Rainwater

Age Group: 3+

Materials Needed: A few different containers that vary in height and width.

What to Do: If it is safe outside but rainy, your child can place the containers on a level surface where they can collect rain and observe which ones fill the fastest (short/shallow/wide versus tall and skinny).

#123 **Activity**: Play in the Rain

Age Group: 2+

Materials Needed: Towel. Optional: rain boots, rain jacket

What to Do: During the summer months, let your child play outside as it rains if there is no threat of lightning. They can be equipped with rain boots and a rain jacket if they desire, or they could be in their swimsuit, an oversized T-shirt, or just their regular clothes. They can jump in puddles, get muddy, or do any exploration that seems fun to them. A bath afterwards is likely to be needed. Use this as an opportunity to talk about where rain comes from and all the benefits it has for the earth.

#124 **Activity**: Mud Painting

Age Group: 2.5+

Materials Needed: A cup, mud, paper, a paintbrush (optional), and a towel for clean-up

What to Do: Just put a scoop of mud into the cup, and let your child paint with it on the paper. They can use a brush, their fingers, or even a small stick if that tickles their fancy.

#125 **Activity**: Rain on Art

Age Group: 2.5+

Materials Needed: Paper towels and markers

What to Do: Put something underneath the paper towel or set it on (dry) concrete outside for your child to color with the markers. Then move the paper towel into the rain so the water can cause the markings to spread and create a whole new piece of art.

#126 **Activity**: Muddy Footprints and Handprints

Age Group: 2+

Materials Needed: Paper, mud, and a towel for cleanup

What to Do: Place the paper nearby on a flat surface so your child can muddy their hands and feet to step on the paper and create handprints and footprints.

PART FOUR
NURTURE

CHAPTER 7
NURTURING CURIOSITY AND LOVE FOR LEARNING

> *We must look to the children as a vehicle for bringing change to humanity.*
>
> MARIA MONTESSORI

t really cannot be overstated: children are extraordinarily capable. A newborn baby needs only to be offered a breast in order to nurse. As the child grows, the parents continue to offer new things, and the child continues to learn and adapt. Children living in the depths of the Amazon jungle will have skills and knowledge specific to their environment that most children of the same age living here in the United States would not possess, and vice versa. On May 1, 2023, a small plane carrying four children and three adults had an engine failure and crashed in a dense Amazonian jungle in the Caquetá Department in Colombia. Two of the adults died on impact; the four children and their mother survived, but the mother succumbed to her injuries after about four days, leaving the children to survive alone for 36 more days before being rescued. Lesly was 13, Soleiny was 9, Tien was 4 at the time of the crash and 5 at the time of the rescue, and Cristin was 11 months old at the time of the crash and 1 at the time of the rescue. The children were members of the Huitoto Indigenous group, and their knowledge and skills of the jungle that were passed down to them from their ancestors enabled them to survive. They had been taught, starting at a very young age, what food is safe and how to protect themselves against the elements. They carried a bag of yuca flour from the plane, and Lesly used water to dissolve it and a leaf to drip it into her baby sister's mouth. In those 40 days, the children would have been battling against constant mosquitoes and flies and were at risk of encountering tarantulas, tapirs, many different kinds of snakes, and other dangers (Otis, 2023). Their survival was miraculous and awe-inspiring. That story is an extreme example of how capable children are and how equipped they can be at young ages to survive the world around them. It is kind and loving towards our children to enable them with the life skills they need to not just survive but to thrive and excel.

MAKE IT FUN

You can see your children's curiosity and natural sense of wonder; it is one of the things that makes parenting so special and fun. There are many things that can interfere with nurturing your child's curiosity. After all, you know the length of your to-do list and the amount of time that would be added to certain tasks if you allowed your child to be a participant in completing the job instead of just completing it on your own.

Aiming to incorporate your children into everyday tasks around the house as much as possible is very encouraged and beneficial, but it is also not feasible to include your child in *every* single task throughout the day. Luckily, there are more ways that we can nurture their curiosity and innate love for learning that are just as encouraged and beneficial. We all know the Barney song, "Clean up, clean up, everybody, everywhere..." No doubt you know how to finish it, "Clean up, clean up, everybody do your share." Why do we sing this song to or with our children? What are we trying to accomplish? We do this to turn a task that can often be seen as mundane into something that is fun. We grasp our child's attention with a tune and begin cleaning in a manner that is upbeat so they can learn that this necessary task can be done with a joyful and positive attitude. Even young babies that cry or protest during diaper and outfit changes are often received by a bouncy, making-up-a-tune, or making-funny-faces parent that is (perhaps subconsciously) teaching their child that everything is okay with the task at hand and that they can have fun together while completing it. When we solely focus on the outcome of what we learn, we lose sight of the joy that can be experienced through the process. This can be seen clearly in many high school and university students who focus so intently on graduation and the degree (the outcome) that they begin to burn out and finish their degree begrudgingly or in "survival mode."

We can combat this by celebrating where our child is while they are there. Jump for joy when your baby pushes to their knees and then immediately pancakes back to the ground. Cheer glee-fully when they swing and miss the ball for the 10th time. Offer a smile and a hug when they express disappointment at a score of 78 on a test they studied hard for. Don't save your expressions of pride just for their successes; let them become accustomed to having fun every step of the way. Make it fun to push, swing, and study so that they continue to push, swing, and study regardless of the results. Do this so that on a random day in February, as a college student who is dizzy from the number of assignments on their plate, your child can remind themselves how far they've come and how much they dreamed of being right where they are. They can remind themselves to enjoy the process because that's what you instilled in them at every stage of their lives, from pushing onto their knees to landing their first big job. This doesn't mean we don't take anything seriously with our kids; there will inevitably be hard conversations or discussions in their upbringing. But we want there to be a safe and secure foundation laid for our children so that they know without a shadow of a doubt that their guardian is *for* them and accepts them as they are. We want them to know that they will be learning new things for the entirety of their lives, and we don't expect them to "arrive" at a certain destination but rather to enjoy being learners and understand that learning is open-ended, not a goal to be obtained.

OPEN-ENDED QUESTIONS

Speaking of open-ended, engaging with your toddler using open-ended questions is another great way to nurture their curiosity. Ask them where they think rain comes from or how we get water to come out of the sink faucet, as well as asking things like "How did you do that?" when they successfully complete some sort of activity. Having them explain to you the process they went through to finish the task will reinforce what they were learning as they did so.

RUSH-FREE ENVIRONMENT

Allowing your child to work in a rush-free environment as much as possible on the tasks they are learning will aid in nurturing their curiosity as they work out issues on their own. Try to make an assessment *before* presenting them with a task on whether or not you think your child can complete it in a certain time frame that is necessary for your upcoming plans. If you know your child will likely not have enough time, it may be best to remove the option to avoid a situation where you let your child start the process and then have to intervene before they finish. This also goes back to what was talked about in Chapter 2 under Self-Care Skills—preparing ahead of time as much as possible to allow your child time and space to dress themselves without having to rush out of the door and not be able to complete the task that they have put their mind to.

OBSERVING AND MIMICKING

One of the signature traits of almost all young kids is that they observe and mimic. This often puts parents in the hot seat since our children are around us and watch us quite a bit, which could lead to something wonderful or something not-so-wonderful. Your child is curious about what you do and will observe and mimic to experience things for themselves. If you wish to nurture their curiosity towards reading, writing, gardening, or any other positive outlet, then let them see you reading, writing, and gardening. If they see you giving your phone, laptop, or TV a lot of your time and attention, then they will want to mimic that and seek out electronics for themselves as well. If you read this and feel a twinge of conviction or fear, please know two things: first, so do I! So does every parent. Second, as mentioned previously, be gentle with yourself. You are not failing—not even close. Every human on the planet will always have some way of growing or improving themselves. Don't be discouraged—just the opposite; take heart and know that any changes you feel you need to make can be made. I'm certain there is at least one other parent in your life who would be willing to make positive changes with you and be a source of accountability if needed. Plus, you can talk openly about these things with your child! This teaches them about self-reflection, which is a crucial part of being an adult, but it also serves as reassurance to your child that perfection (as a person) is not the goal. When your child feels that they must be perfect to get your or society's approval, it can be detrimental to their self-confidence. So don't hold back; let your child be a part of your journey to make healthy changes and explain why you desire to do so.

LEARNING STYLES

Research on different learning styles has become much more in-depth over the last few decades. Some people are auditory and enjoy learning through listening, and they may enjoy audiobooks. Other people are visual learners and prefer to see diagrams and pictures. Whereas others are tactile learners who need to physically place their hands on objects and manipulate them to take in the information through touch. Then, there are learners who prefer to absorb content through reading and writing. These are the four most predominant learning styles observed, but there are layers beyond them, such as preferences for being solitary to learn or in a more social setting. There are also people who present a certain knack for logic and mathematics, which is often set apart from visual, auditory, kinesthetic, and reading/writing. People can easily be a combination of styles as well. Take note of what you notice in your toddler and try to appeal to their learning style. This will increase their love for learning if they can be at ease with the way the content is presented. Along with caring for their learning style, we also want to follow our child's interests and passions as they grow. If your child is showing strength in a particular area, run with that and press in further instead of simply moving on because they have shown mastery. Sometimes, our first instinct is to help our child improve on their weaknesses, but many times when we focus on their strengths instead, their confidence will be boosted, and they may find within themselves a way to tackle the challenges they have on a different subject. This positive reinforcement can spur our child's love for learning to the point where they carry it into adulthood.

ABSTRACT CONCEPTS AND CREATIVE SOLUTIONS

Many of the things we teach our children are abstract concepts, such as thankfulness. Consider the Hamel family and how their tradition around the Thanksgiving holiday nurtures a love for learning thankfulness in a tangible and special way for their children. Starting on the 1st leading up to Thanksgiving Day and continuing until the 30th, this family takes time every evening for each family member to share something they are grateful for, and mom documents it on a large whiteboard for the whole month. Considering they are a family of six, the board begins bursting with all the many things they are thankful for as they try not to repeat any of their answers or to have the same answers as their family members. This gives them a visual representation of the quantity of blessings that can't necessarily be seen with their eyes, such as, "Today I was thankful that my sister helped me find my lost shoe." This tradition expands their situational awareness as they try to give unique answers and promotes attitudes of gratitude.

When you incorporate your child into day-to-day household activities, they will have a sense of purpose on top of all the other benefits previously discussed. This sense of purpose ties into their love for learning and innate curiosity about the world, as they will seek out ways to build upon the purpose they feel and see what else they can accomplish. Providing opportunities for your child to progress from transferring liquid from a measuring cup into a pot, to pouring liquids directly from a container, to displaying safety with taking a tray out of the oven, all the way to following a recipe from beginning to end and cooking dinner for the family, will allow for their purpose to deepen—not just within the family but as a member of society as well. An example from another family, the Doe family, comes to mind when their four kids were teenagers, and they had a 5th teenager, a foreign exchange student from Japan, also living in their home. The mom was cooking quite a lot to keep up with so many people and began to brainstorm ideas to help alleviate her burden. Her creative solution was to assign each teenager a day out of the week, Monday-Friday, where they were to cook dinner for the family, and she primarily focused on cooking over the weekends. She would help her kids find recipes if they wanted, and she would also help them in the kitchen if they had any questions. This setup worked out wonderfully, and she was able to bond with her teens one-on-one creating fun memories and also instilling valuable lifelong skills. They were also able to learn more about Japanese culture through some dishes that their Japanese sister made, and likewise, she also received a cultural experience by choosing to cook some American cuisine. Her children, who are now grown, have talked about how memorable that time-frame was for them and how grateful they are to have practiced so much cooking before moving out on their own.

THE POWER OF NATURE

The world has so much that can be explored. Remember that your personal love for learning, exploring, and displaying curiosity will rub off on your children. Be a participant with them as you plan excursions and seek to expose them to muse-ums, nature walks, science experiments, and all sorts of field trips. Encourage your child to ask questions and to maintain a perspective of ongoing discovery and curiosity. Being out in nature is especially helpful for stirring up questions in your children since there are big and little wonders nearly every-where we turn, even in the simple park up the street. Being in nature and exploring it with curiosity has been shown to boost creativity, reduce stress, increase physical activity, improve mental health, and enhance learning (Asher, 2023). Any way you can increase the amount of time you spend with your kids outside will be beneficial to their well-being. Think back on your own childhood and the wonder you felt being outdoors, as well as any impactful memories that are linked to nature. Let this be fuel for you as a parent to ensure that your children have a deep love for and connection with nature. Especially in today's time when technology is bursting all around us. It's easy to forget about how much noise humans create and are subjected to in today's world, specifically unnatural noises such as trains, planes, cars, TVs, ticking clocks, or the hum of the AC.

When we get deep enough into nature, those noises fade away, and we can turn our ears to the peaceful sounds of Mother Nature instead. We can breathe in fresh air and begin to intentionally relax. Maybe you don't have a way to get that deep into nature on a regular basis (though that's a fantastic goal!), but even sitting in an outdoor space that is available to you still brings a sense of peace that can be difficult to match through other outlets. For our children, maybe they aren't all that still when they are in nature at first, but through your loving guidance, we can teach them to perk up their ears and concentrate their eyes to see the parts of nature that hide when we're loud and moving around but begin to creep out for us to see when we're still and quiet. The world is busy, and without intentionality on our part, we can get swept up in the hustle and bustle very quickly. We have a duty to guard our children from the hustle and bustle and teach them the importance of being still and quiet so that, as adults, they are able to do it for themselves.

Even with all the ways we strive to parent positively and have peace between us and our children or between siblings, there will still be moments of conflict, disobedience, and rebellion in some shape, form, or level. It is immensely helpful to have a solid understanding of what you, your partner, and other active participants in rearing your child are aiming for in terms of discipline and routine. You want to be on the offensive side of parenting, not the defensive side. Explore the next chapter to see if any of the strategies would be beneficial in your home.

CHAPTER 8
PRACTICAL STRATEGIES FOR EVERYDAY LIFE

> *It is through the activity of the child that the mind of man is created. We must consider, therefore, the child – who has this power, this activity, who is the builder of man, who is a spiritual embryo.*

> MARIA MONTESSORI

As we've seen throughout this book, there are a lot of things that our sweet little humans are learning during their childhood, especially in those first three years of life. The primary focus of this book is not on discipline, but there are some strategies that are worth discussing, along with the importance of structure and routine for your toddler. Some of these concepts have already been lightly sprinkled through the previous chapters but are being reinforced here. The concepts mentioned are options that have been proven effective, and that is why they are being discussed, not because they are "the right or only way." You alone can determine the course you take with disciplining your child, and these things are only being shared so that you can have another tool in your toolbox if you so desire.

UNDERSTANDING CONSEQUENCES

A note on the word *consequence* that will appear a few times: There are major differences between the meanings of the words *consequence* and *punishment*. All actions taken by people have consequences, which means that the word itself is neither positive nor negative; it is neutral. Unfortunately, in today's time, it is usually only used in a negative context for bad behavior. Try to normalize the use of the word in positive contexts as well so that your child does not link the meaning of consequence to that of punishment. Punishments are negative and produce guilt, shame, and even fear. We do not want our children to be obedient out of fear; we want them to learn for themselves the joys of being obedient because of the positive consequences that flow from their good behavior and choices. If it is possible to utilize a natural consequence, that is ideal. Natural consequences are usually more impactful than something you or I might come up with, but nonetheless, it is wise to have some set consequences in place that are known to your child, such as timeouts. For example, if your toddler is yanking on the curtains in the bedroom, and this is the first time you know of them doing so, you intervene and explain that pulling on the curtains is not allowed, and if they do it again, then they will have a timeout. First offenses do not warrant a consequence, as we instead give our child the benefit of the doubt that they did not know what they were doing was wrong. A natural consequence in this scenario with the curtains could potentially be the curtain rod breaking and falling atop the child, which could then lead to an injury; but since we don't want our child to go through that kind of experience, nor do we want to let them continue the behavior until the worst-case scenario happens, we instead use a consequence of our choosing to impact the child enough to make them understand that repeating the behavior is a bad idea. This is a loving and kind thing to do for our children.

Consequences should also not be a surprise to the child; they should be told exactly what the consequence will be for repeating the behavior with language that helps them understand that it is their choice. "Mommy does not want you pulling on the curtains because it is dangerous, and you could get hurt. If you do it again, you will go to timeout. If you choose to pull on the curtains again, you are choosing to take a timeout. If you choose to leave the curtains alone, then you are choosing to continue to play with your toys and not go to timeout." Additionally, try to observe your child's behavior to see if you can come up with a way to satisfy the need they are displaying. In this case, the child wanted to engage in the motion of yanking on the curtain. Is there a way you can create an activity that involves a yanking motion for your child that would be appropriate? "The first idea that a child must acquire in order to be actively disciplined is the difference between right and wrong, and it is the duty of the instructor to prevent the child from confusing immobility with good and activity with evil, as happened with the old kind of discipline. It is our object to train the child for activity, for work, for doing good, and not for immobility or passivity" (Maria Montessori 150, n.d.).

Montessori philosophy aims to keep discipline positive and seeks to understand the underlying causes of unwanted behavior in a child so that they can be helped to express themselves in a way that allows them to fit in with their peers, which is an innate human quality that the child longs for (Montessori Kids Universe, 2020). In her book, *My First 300 Babies*, author Glayds Hendrick makes the point that it is not about what the child does but how you (the parent or guardian) respond to it (Gladys West Hendrick, 1999) Babies and kids can be unpredictable, but our response doesn't have to be. Although we still want to view and treat our child as the unique individual that they are, we also want them to form habits that serve them in the family unit and in society. Habits such as having respect for authority, kindness towards all people, and polite manners. These kinds of habits can be a struggle for many toddlers because it can be difficult for them to understand the why behind what makes these behaviors appropriate and accepted. They are still in the early stages of figuring out how to cope with their emotions and how to choose certain behaviors even when they don't "feel" like it. We can help them by speaking about how we are each in control of our own attitudes, even when we are happy, sad, or mad. How we can feel those emotions and still choose which words come out of our mouths and what we do with our hands and feet. Validate their feelings while encouraging them to make good choices in the midst of difficult emotions.

One very last comment on consequences: Make them realistic and not empty threats. If your children are bickering and fighting over a portable DVD player in the car while on a road trip, do not say, "If you don't stop arguing, I will throw the whole thing out the window!" unless you truly intend to follow through on that sort of hefty consequence. We do not want to form a habit of lying to our children with wild consequences that we would never actually do; this diminishes our word, and children begin to quickly pick up on whether such statements are too intense to be true.

DEFIANCE RELATED OUTBURSTS

First and foremost: Applying the first seven chapters of the content of this book (especially what is in Chapter 2) will result in a toddler finding security and independence, which then has a direct effect on their emotional well-being. That means emotional outbursts will already be decreasing as they strengthen their ability to self-regulate in the Montessori atmosphere. Emotional outbursts can happen for several reasons, and almost all scenarios are able to be handled without consequences if we are properly diagnosing the reason for the behavior and able to provide an outlet for the child. This is what we want to aim for instead of turning to consequence-giving when the child is actually in need of a way to explore properly or try something new. Even with a significant number of outbursts decreasing or being quickly diminished with proper assessment, there is still one specific type of outburst that has the potential to occur that we want to look at a little differently and offer a solution that, as mentioned, has proven effective in many homes. Outbursts stemming from a place of defiance are arguably the hardest type for parents to handle. Having respect for our child does not mean that they have a license to do whatever they want or to tell you or other adults "no" when told (not asked) to do something. I want to be especially clear on the type of scenario that we are looking into. There are acceptable and respectful ways for children to request doing something differently or requesting (not demanding) not to do something that their parents have told them to do. Having an outburst of screaming, crying, yelling, crossing arms and pouting, declaring "no!" or arguing, or a combination of those things, in response to being given a direct command is not acceptable or respectful behavior. It is important to stick to your word once you have given your child directions on something (as well as to be picky about when you do).

What we have seen is that consistently and immediately holding your ground, kindly but firmly, is the fastest way to combat tantrum-throwing behavior or backtalk. If your child protests against you and the result is that they get what they want and not what you directed them to do, then they are learning that throwing a fit is to their benefit. If you attempt to explain afterwards why that kind of behavior is unacceptable, it will not land because they walked away "victorious." They have no logical reason why their behavior would be unacceptable when they had nothing but good feelings afterwards. Instead, if a child protests and the parent holds firm to see that their direction is followed and then gives a consequence (that was set ahead of time) for the child defiantly protesting, then the child walks away with a much more logical understanding that their behavior was unacceptable since they did not get their way and reaped the preset consequence. They will want to avoid that behavior moving forward so as not to endure the same series of events.

Does this work to resolve defiant outbursts the very first time that the child protests and the parent stands firm? Heavens no, the child is learning a concept, and concepts take some time. Just as your child cannot learn the alphabet by hearing it one time, he cannot learn to control emotional outbursts after one instance. Instead, we sing the alphabet and practice the letters multiple times a day for several weeks until, one day, our child has it down all on their own. The repetition to learn the alphabet is for a very short timeframe of the child's overall life; dealing with defiant-related tantrums can be just as isolated if we are diligent in their young years when the protests begin to happen. Furthermore, when we practice the alphabet with our child, we say the letters in the same order every time; we do not mix them around and present it differently each time, as this would drastically slow down their ability to learn it. If you deal with defiant outbursts differently each time they occur, sometimes standing firm, other times giving in, and having inconsistent or differing consequences, then the child is delayed in learning that their defiance will not be tolerated.

Family A may have a different "alphabet" than Family B for how they choose to handle defiant outbursts, but both families are consistent with how they've set up their "alphabet," and their respective children learn it through the consistent repetition. The sooner your child accepts that his or her parents and guardians are the authority figures and not themselves, the sooner they will settle into the safe and secure structure of the home you have created for them. This is to their benefit and meets their intrinsic needs. If they spend years, sometimes winning tantrums but other times losing, they will be confused as to the structure of the home and continue to lash out since there is an internal insecurity that is not being resolved. This continual back and forth can lead to such exhaustion for the parents that they move towards standing their ground less and less, which teaches the child that their behavior is acceptable and effective for getting their way. This eventually turns into elementary-aged kids and teenagers who may not even go through the effort or display of a tantrum but rather just ignore their parent and do what they please, and the parent appears to have gotten to the point of shrugging it off or laughing it off (if a witness is present) as "kids will be kids." When faced with a toddler who is being defiant against you, be firm but kind when you speak to them; it should not be a screaming match. We are modeling for them the respect that we want them to have for us. As mentioned at the start, we respect the child and the fact that they are free to express themselves or have differing opinions or desires from us, but they need guidance in how to express themselves respectfully and have conversations instead of throwing a fit or arguing. The "conversations" might initially be one-sided as we consider our toddler's lack of language acquisition, but they can still nod yes and no as you guide a respectful conversation about what your toddler was trying to express after having handled the outburst. There is a common phrase among parents nowadays that goes like this: "Pick your battles." This is good advice under the right circumstances, and

I would say to lean on it only under this condition: That you and your child have not yet entered into a battle. Meaning that if you have yet to engage with your child on something that you think may lead to a defiance-related meltdown, then perhaps don't "pick" it—your toddler will never know that you have avoided a battle—but the moment you engage with your child with a command, and they respond on any level with a protest or rebellion, you have thus entered "the battle." To not choose it once it is already occurring means that your child is the victor by default. Unfortunately, some of these battles will take longer than a few seconds to resolve. You will have to see to it that your direction is followed, and that may mean moving the protesting child to a solitary place until they are calm and then trying again. Work to be mindful of what your toddler may have going on within them before you give them a command, and aim to withhold direct commands unless you intend for your child to be obedient to it.

Again, please keep in mind everything else we have discussed up to this point, and don't just read that last section in isolation. We must remember that this sensitive time with our toddlers is largely because of their pursuit of independence. Your child can be independent *and* respect authority. That is what we try to teach them since it is part of being a functional adult one day. As noted, not all tantrums, meltdowns, or protests are directly linked to fighting against you as an authority figure; in fact, most of them are not. Take the time to recognize what fueled your child's behavior before reacting as if they are being defiant. This means not responding to your child's behavior out of your emotions but looking deeper into what the child's behavior means and not how the behavior makes you feel. We don't want to turn to giving a consequence for an outburst that was due to not being able to get their left shoe onto their foot; instead, we want to offer comfort, encouragement, and praise for how hard they tried and point out their success in getting the other shoe on without help. Then discuss how they made the choice to scream and throw their shoe when they felt frustrated, when they had the power and the self-control to instead come and calmly ask for help, even if they were upset that they couldn't do it on their own. This acknowledges their emotions and shows them that they always have options, even when feeling strong emotions. Remind yourself to assume the best of your child before reacting to what they are doing, which may seem belligerent on the outside. If you are very near your child when you see a strong emotion coming over them, try to get down face to face, place a hand on their chest, lock eyes, and say "deep breath" while letting them see you take a big breath. You can also put their hand on your chest so they can feel the inhale and join in with you. After practicing this a number of times over a number of days, your child will begin to take a deep breath as their first reaction to a big emotion instead of turning to an outburst. This is also wonderful advice for us as parents as we navigate the emotional rollercoaster that is parenthood. Remember to breathe and not take yourself too seriously; this stage goes by much too quickly.

BRIBES AND EXTERNAL REWARDS

Try to aim for a middle ground in your discipline techniques. Allow enough freedom for your child to safely explore while still having set rules and boundaries that are clear for your child. Using bribes or excess external rewards for good behavior can be problematic down the line because it does not mirror what your child will experience as an adult-student or in the workplace. We want our children to respect others, have a strong work ethic, and have a deep sense of right and wrong that is produced from within them and not from a place of doing good to receive candy or a desired physical item and avoiding bad to dodge uncomfortable consequences. We want completed tasks to be rewarding in and of themselves. Consider how, as an adult in a professional work environment, the primary benefit of respecting one's boss and having integrity in their work is that they *keep their job*. Not necessarily to get a bonus, which may occasionally occur and is a nice thing, but to expect a bonus or some sort of regular reward for all the things we do well at our job blinds us from the blessing that it is just to have the job at all and to be a dependable, honest employee that is providing for themselves or their family. The Montessori term *Discipline from Within* applies here, "The discipline in a well-run Montessori classroom is not a result of the teacher's control or of rewards or punishments. Its source comes from within each individual child, who can control his or her own actions and make positive choices regarding personal behavior" (Association Montessori Internationale, n.d.).

ORDER, ROUTINE, AND TRANSITIONS

Having routine and order in one's home allows a child to relax into the environment and feel safe and secure as they set out to learn about the world around them each day. This requires us as parents to be organized, plan ahead, and be equipped to handle unexpected turns of events so that reorienting back to the schedule is as quick and smooth as possible. Children who have a deep sense of security are happy. A child who is operating out of fear or insecurity may have obvious meltdowns or turn to isolation as a way to cope. Some children also express higher needs for routine and order than others. My friend's adult daughter was a nanny for three children for four and a half years and noticed how one of the three kids would sometimes get overly hyper to the point of being out of control when they would go places. The more she paid attention to it, the more the pattern seemed to be any spur-of-the-moment outings where the boy would be acting up the most. She then realized further that there were often outings and plans that she, as the caretaker, knew about days beforehand, or at least a day or two beforehand, that she simply kept to herself and would tell the kids about as she had them getting ready to go or once they were in the car and on the way. This made it feel like a "spur of the moment" to them, even though that wasn't her intention. She decided to start sharing more with the children about their plans for the upcoming week, especially engaging with the boy and answering any questions he had about what they would be up to. "...And my goodness! He did have quite a lot of questions!" she told me. She would remind them about what was going on and what they could expect as plans drew nearer and the boy had a drastic change in his behavior while they were out.

He needed time to think, envision, and anticipate things so he could feel more in control of himself. Most children are this way on some level. Having oversized calendars, charts, and lists that are visible day-to-day for your children to see or interact with will aid in this pursuit of order and routine in the home. This goes hand in hand with any and all transitions your child will experience as they age. If you are looking to smoothly transition your child into a Montessori preschool environment or from Montessori into a traditional kindergarten setting, begin having conversations about the changes well ahead of time with your child. Ask questions about what they think it will be like and answer any questions they may have about the teachers, other students, or the activities they might do. Point out and discuss the positives and all the things that make this change exciting. Communicate with and get to know the teachers ahead of time, and see if your child can visit them in person at least once, if not more before the transition takes place. After the transition, maintain regular communication with the teachers, be observant of your child's behavior, and listen to everything they have to say about the new environment. Whether going to or from Montessori or traditional education, work to incorporate some activities into your home that mimics what your child will be exposed to at their school so there is less "culture shock."

The Montessori Philosophy is meant to be easily incorporated into the family because it seeks to develop real-life skills in children. It is meant to be practical and extremely applicable since the aim is to bring our children alongside us in partici-pating in society. There are many families out there that have brought Montessori thinking into their home and are so relieved to experience a new level of joy with their children as they self-regulate and display kindness and unique capabilities. You and your toddler are not alone on this journey. Find like-minded families near you to collaborate with, especially if there is not a Montessori school in your area or if it is not possible to utilize the ones that are. Plan outings and field trips with other families so you can work together and enjoy your children in your community. Utilize today's technology to find local groups to connect with that may have social media platforms you can join or follow.

Here is just a short list of websites you can reference for more ways to support bringing Montessori into your home:

- www.tlvschool.com/parent-corner
- www.themontessorinotebook.com/free-resources
- www.trilliummontessori.org/resources-for-montessori-teachers/
- www.carrotsareorange.com/ultimate-list-montessori-assessment-tools-resources
- www.montessori-ami.org/resource-library/facts/glossary-montessori-terms

KEEP THE MONTESSORI MAGIC ALIVE

Now that you've equipped yourself to embrace Montessori parenting, it's time to pay it forward and guide other readers to discover the same invaluable knowledge.

By sharing your authentic thoughts about this book on Amazon, you'll be guiding other parents toward the wealth of information they seek, passing forward your passion for the Montessori philosophy.

Thank you for your assistance. The Montessori Philosophy thrives when we share our wisdom and you're playing a vital role in that journey.

With heartfelt gratitude,
Your ally, Amy Lee Terres

CONCLUSION

> *The child does not work in order to move or in order to become intelligent. He works to adapt to his environment. It is essential that he has many experiences in the environment if he is to do this.*

MARIA MONTESSORI

> *It is not that man must develop in order to work, but that man must work in order to develop.*

MARIA MONTESSORI

Putting the content of this book into practice looks like becoming an observer of your toddler and paying close attention to how they operate in different settings and the strengths that they display. Remind yourself often that your child is naturally wired to learn and explore the world so they can see that they have a place in it. This will give them deep satisfaction and teach them how to self-regulate and interact with their peers and authority figures. The 12 principles of Montessori Philosophy will come to life as you watch your child through this lens and see all the ways that they align with your child's behavior and reap desired consequences when applied. This sensitive period of language acquisition makes our toddlers a little more limited in expressing themselves through articulate speech, but you will know through their body language and behavior how much they are enjoying the Montessori changes. You will see your child problem-solving independently, regulating their emotions, and tending to younger children with an eagerness to help them with something they have mastered.

You get a thrill watching them master their fine and gross motor skills through the activities you have lovingly prepared and presented to them. Their cognitive development will be directly affected by the activities as well as the changes in how you interact with and relate to your child after applying the principles. You will begin to see each space in your home differently and come up with many more ideas to involve your toddler in daily tasks. Your connection with nature will increase right along with your child's connection as you explore together and take in the never-ending wonders. Normalize "Montessori parenthood" in your home; make it for you just as much as for your kids. Your child's inner security will skyrocket as you display kind yet firm discipline on a regular basis so that they don't experience confusion. They will lose interest in protesting against the commands you give as they understand more and more that you respect them and love them unconditionally. Your toddler will feel seen and valued as they actively participate in the home. Now is the time to take charge of your parenting approach and unlock the full potential of your toddler. You are equipped with the tools and knowledge to create a home environment that supports your child's growth, development, and lifelong love of learning. Join the Montessori movement and discover the joy of witnessing your toddler blossom into a confident, independent, and compassionate individual. Embrace the principles that have guided generations of parents and educators and witness their transformative impact on your family dynamics. Don't miss this opportunity to create a lasting bond with your toddler while providing them with the foundations for a successful future. The toddler years go by so quickly. Do all you can to soak it up with your child. They are your biggest fans and long for your presence as they figure out just who they are in this big and wondrous world.

GROUP GAMES + PARTY IDEAS

Is your house where all the neighborhood kids come to play? Need some game ideas for your child's next birthday party? Here is a quick reference for some fun activities.

Cut the Cake: Children stand in a circle facing inwards and holding hands. One child walks around on the outside of the circle and "cuts the cake" by choosing to "slice" two of the children's hands that are joined together. The two children that got sliced each take off running in the opposite direction around the circle while the slicer stands in the gap of the circle with his hands out to his side. The child that makes it around the circle and grabs the slicer's hand first is safe and joins back into the circle; the other is now the new slicer that begins walking around to choose the next victims.

Pair Up Tag: Instead of one person being "it," everyone is linked arms with another person in groups of two as they run around and must coordinate together to avoid being tagged.

Freeze Tag: You can have several variations of freeze tag, such as crawling under people's legs to unfreeze them, using cut pool noodles to unfreeze people, standing face to face with a frozen person and spelling their name to unfreeze them, etc.

Relay Races: Get creative!

Slip 'n Slide: You can make your own with a tarp, water hose, and slippery soap

I Declare War: Four players who each choose whatever country they want to be. Draw an extra-large circle with a piece of chalk or, with a large stick, draw the circle in the dirt (if no concrete is available). Section off for each player—USA, Canada, Spain, and India—everyone stands in their section; Spain throws a stick into Canada's territory, then Spain, USA, and India take off running away from Canada's direction as fast as they can while Canada runs to get the stick that was thrown in their section. Once Canada has the stick, they yell HALT! and all the running countries stop moving. Canada uses an under-hand throw of the stick to try and hit the country of their choice (whoever they think they can successfully hit). In this case, Canada chooses India; if Canada succeeds in hitting India (the actual person) with the stick, they take the chalk (or stick for dirt), and without moving their feet or letting their stomach touch the ground, they take as much of India's territory as they can. If Canada throws the stick and misses India, then India gets to take as much territory as it can from Canada. Then, the next round starts with Canada throwing the stick into whichever territory they choose.

Hide The Rock: Stand in a circle facing inwards with one person in the middle, show the person in the middle who has the rock in their hand, and then start playing music. Everyone in the circle moves their fists from their neighbors' fists to their own chests. The person in the middle is trying to follow where the rock goes while everyone is moving their fisted hands up and down continuously and discreetly moving the rock into their neighbor's hands, transferring it to their other hand (if they choose) so they can keep passing it. The rock can change direction at any point. When the music stops, the person in the middle guesses who has the rock.

Human Knot: Stand in a circle facing inward; everyone reaches out their hands and grabs the hands of two other people, arms crossing in all directions. Get untangled without anyone having to let go at any point.

Classics:

- Musical Chairs
- LeapFrog
- Ring Around The Rosie
- Duck, Duck, Goose
- Tug-a-War

- Red Light, Green Light
- Simon Says
- Limbo
- Heads Up 7 Up
- Sharks and Minos
- Marco Polo
- Kickball
- Jump Rope
- Hula Hooping
- Hot Potato
- Water Balloon Sheet Toss
- Water Balloon Fight
- Flying Kites
- Wall Ball
- Red Rover

REFERENCES

12 Select Principles of Montessori Education - GMN. Welcome to the Global Montessori Network, 24 Aug. 2022, theglobalmontessorinetwork.org/12-select-principles-of-montessori-education/.

Anthony, D. (2017, March 27). *Famous Montessori Student Success Stories.* Primary Montessori. https://primarymontessori.com/famous-montessori-student-success-stories/

Asher, H. (2023, April 29). *The Importance of Curiosity and Nature Connection.* An Darach Forest Therapy. https://silvotherapy.co.uk/articles/increasing-curiosity-and-nature-connection

Association Montessori Internationale. (n.d.). *Glossary of Montessori Terms.* Association Montessori Internationale. https://montessori-ami.org/resource-library/facts/glossary-montessori-terms

Engler, B. (2021, October 12). *Building Conflict Resolution Skills in Children.* Connections Academy. https://www.connectionsacademy.com/support/resources/article/building-conflict-resolution-skills-in-children/

Gladys West Hendrick. (1999). *My First 300 Babies.* Hurst Pub.

Lillard AS, Meyer MJ, Vasc D and Fukuda E (2021) *An Association Between Montessori Education in Childhood and Adult Wellbeing.* Front Psychol. 12:721943. doi: https://10.3389/fpsyg.2021.721943

Maria Montessori 150. (n.d.). *Montessori Quotes | Montessori 150.* Maria Montessori 150. https://montessori150.org/maria-montessori/montessori-quotes

Montessori Kids Universe. (2020, January 13). *Positive Discipline and the Montessori Method for Raising Children.* Montessori Kids Universe. https://montessorikidsuniverse.com/positive-discipline-montessori-cheat-sheet/

Otis, J. (2023, June 17). *How Indigenous kids survived 40 days in Colombia's jungle after a plane crash.* NPR. https://www.npr.org/2023/06/17/1182715412/colombia-rescue-plane-crash-indigenous-children

Viktoria. (2020, April 17). *Setting Up a Montessori Classroom.* Get Brainy Box. https://getbrainybox.com/setting-up-a-montessori-classroom/

What is sensory play and why is it important? (2022, February 10). Action for

Children. https://www.actionforchildren.org.uk/blog/what-is-sensory-play-and-why-is-it-important/

Made in the USA
Monee, IL
03 March 2024

54062421R00105